CREATING A SPEAKING AND LISTENING CLASSROOM

Providing children with opportunities to talk about their learning enables teachers to hear what children are thinking. Talking with one another allows children to question, elaborate and reflect on a range of ideas. Classroom talk can be motivating and involving, and helps children to think and learn. And yet it is difficult to organise such talk in a classroom. Children unaware of the importance of talk for learning may think of talk as 'just chat' – and learning falls away as they slip into social talk. This book provides teachers with strategies and resources to enable whole classes to work together through the medium of talk.

Creating a Speaking and Listening Classroom provides timely professional development for teachers. Based on a theoretical approach underpinned by classroom research, this book offers classroom-tested strategies for engaging children in their own learning. Such strategies involve the direct teaching of speaking and listening. Activities in the book can ensure that children know how and why to support one another's learning in whole-class and group work. The approach enables teachers to ensure that personalised learning programmes are based on what children already think and know. The suggested strategies for teaching speaking and listening can enable children to use one another's minds as a rich resource.

This stimulating book will be of interest to professionals in primary education, literacy co-ordinators and trainee primary teachers.

Lyn Dawes is a leading authority on speaking and listening in the primary classroom. A former primary school teacher, Lyn is currently a science education lecturer at the University of Northampton. She is author of *The Essential Speaking and Listening*, also published by Routledge.

CREATING A SPEAKING AND LISTENING CLASSROOM

Integrating talk for learning at Key Stage 2

Lyn Dawes

Illustrated by Lynne Breeze

Routledge
Taylor & Francis Group

LONDON AND NEW YORK

This first edition published 2011
by Routledge
2 Park Square, Milton Park, Abingdon, Oxon, OX14 4RN

Simultaneously published in the USA and Canada
by Routledge
270 Madison Avenue, New York, NY 10016

Routledge is an imprint of the Taylor & Francis Group, an informa business

© 2011 Lyn Dawes

Typeset in Helvetica Neue by
Florence Production Ltd, Stoodleigh, Devon
Printed and bound in Great Britain by
MPG Books Group, UK

British Library Cataloguing in Publication Data
A catalogue record for this book is available from the British Library

Library of Congress Cataloging-in-Publication Data
Dawes, Lyn.
  Creating a speaking and listening classroom: integrating talk for
  learning at key stage 2/by Lyn Dawes. – 1st ed.
      p. cm.
  1. Oral communication – Study and teaching (Elementary).
  2. Listening – Study and teaching (Elementary).   3. Classroom
  environment.   I. Title.
  LB1572.D38 2011
  372.62'2 – dc22   2010008377

ISBN13: 978–0–415–48151–9 (pbk)
ISBN13: 978–0–203–84479–3 (ebk)

This book is for Derwent, Betsy, Poppy and Maia, with love.

CONTENTS

ACKNOWLEDGMENTS

The Thinking Together team of Neil Mercer, Rupert Wegerif, Claire Sams, Karen Littleton and Judith Kleine Staarman provided the inspiration for the contents of this book. They helped me to see the importance of this work and to understand what it offers children. Their research provides evidence that teaching children how to discuss things with one another helps them to think and learn. It's a great team and I am proud to be part of it.

My University of Northampton science colleagues, Babs Dore, Linda Nicholls and Peter Loxely, provided a constant source of creative ideas and implemented ideas with enthusiasm and conviction. I have been very grateful for this and for Linda's invaluable comments on Chapters 4 and 8 – I have used some of her sentences as she will see! Penny Coltman (Cambridge) kindly provided the insight for section 5 of Chapter 3. Paul Warwick and Sylvia Wolfe (Cambridge) and Barbara Leedham (Bedford) have invariably been interested in and supportive of Thinking Together and I would like to thank them. Senior management and teachers at Water Hall School, Milton Keynes, especially Tony Draper and Karen Roberts, have shown a continuing and practical interest in Thinking Together. Thank you to Anna Mercer for proofreading and finding no mistakes.

At Routledge I would like to thank Bruce Roberts and James Hobbs for their patience and support. I would also like to thank all the children who have been involved in the research and trialling of materials. Thank you also to Lynne for the beautiful illustrations which capture the essence of childhood. Finally I would like to thank Neil for his conviction that the book should, could and would be written, and for what he said about Chapter 3, and all the constant help.

Lyn Dawes
January 2010

INTRODUCTION

Talk for learning

Usually, children start learning to talk as soon as they are part of a conversation – that is, as soon as they arrive. Children's first attempts to copy what they hear may be amusing approximations, often better than the original. Our smallest family member has introduced the word *cupperty* into the house vocabulary, and no doubt we will still be embarrassing her by 'having a cupperty' when she is quite grown up. This is one way words mutate and evolve. We learn to speak by hearing and using words. Children constantly try out words and creative combinations of words. So, most children can say a lot about themselves and the world they live in by the time they reach school. They can name and describe things, listen to others, assimilate and creatively use new vocabulary, and even switch between languages, all with astonishing facility. It appears that talk just comes naturally.

Maybe it is because children have this seemingly effortless capacity to speak and listen – that is, talk – that this area of their development has been given low priority at school. Some schools do teach public speaking, debating, reading aloud, improvisation and other dramatic techniques. Most teachers encourage children to talk to partners, the whole class, the adults working in the room, and sometimes even the whole school. But usually mention of talk is to do with behaviour. Understandably, we teachers often ask children to stop talking; if 30 or so children are all trying to speak, no one can listen, think or learn. Sometimes children do just want to chatter about their own concerns and it's lovely to hear them. But our job as professionals is to ensure that there is a direction to learning. The problem for teachers is that of balance; we are aware that children need to talk. Children need chances to express their own ideas and listen to different points of view, to talk through problems or share ideas to create something new. In order to do this effectively, children really need direct tuition of key speaking and listening skills. We assume that children know how to discuss ideas at our peril. If they are to make the most of classroom opportunities to learn, we must teach them how to talk to one another, and why: as Sir Jim Rose (Rose, 2008: 7 (see Websites)) puts it:

> Due attention must be given to the prime skills of speaking and listening as essential in their own right and crucial for learning to read, write, to be numerate and, indeed, to be successful in virtually all of the learning children undertake at school and elsewhere.

Children need to say things aloud if they are to check their own understanding and that of others. They need to hear what their classmates think. But in classrooms, how can we encourage talk without generating chaotic noise? How can children discuss ideas or talk creatively without slipping into too much casual social chatter? What sort of talk will help children to develop their thinking and support their learning? How can we ensure that children hear reasoned discussion, so that they can take part themselves?

We can aim to create a speaking and listening classroom – an environment where children voice their ideas, ask questions and listen to one another talking about ideas in ways that will help them to develop their thinking.

This book examines some classroom talk, and describes strategies which can encourage meaningful talk and which can be adapted for use across the curriculum.

Chapter 1

TALK TOOLKITS OF TEACHERS AND CHILDREN

The idea of talk as a 'tool' for use in learning originated in the early twentieth century in the writings of Lev Vygotsky. Vygotsky realised that we use tools to think – that is, that words and speech are metaphorical tools put to use to develop and communicate understanding. We can take this idea – that language acts as a 'set of tools' – to analyse the 'talk toolkit' of teachers. For teachers, talk is really the main tool of the trade. But what talk tools are effective in terms of teaching and learning? It is evident to any classroom observer that some teacher talk is of immense benefit for learners, and some is a hopeless waste of time.

The next section offers examples of talk from primary classrooms, so that we can consider what is more, or less, effective in terms of teaching and learning. Before reflecting on these snippets from classroom life, it's important to note that although it is very easy to point out how to teach, it is very difficult to actually do it. Yet most teachers are extremely good at their job. Their creativity, commitment and enthusiasm help children to learn day after day in schools. Such expertise is generated over time as teachers constantly reflect on their practice; self evaluation (often rather negative!) is a characteristic of the profession. The examples from classrooms included here are intended to contribute to developing practice. I offer no support to those who blame teachers for the ills of the education system in general, or children's problems and difficulties with learning in particular.

The teacher's toolkit: some ineffective talk

Transcript 1: Triangles is an example of a teacher (T) at work. Year 3 children are seated on a carpet around the teacher in a low chair. The Learning Intention for the lesson is: 'To use everyday language to describe features of familiar 3-D shapes'.

We can consider what talk tools this teacher is using, and to what effect.

Transcript 1: Triangles

T:	Right, OK. You guys. I wonder who, um, can anybody tell me what we did in Numeracy last week? *(five hands go up)*
T:	Blake?
Blake:	Traditional tales?
T:	No, listen, numeracy. Numbers. What did we do? Anyone? *(still the same hands up)* Come on, you were all there. Polly? *(Polly does not have her hand up)*
Polly:	Triangles?

T:	Right! Shape is what we were doing, 2-D shapes, and last week we looked at triangles. What is important about a triangle? *(few hands are up)* Tamar sit on your bottom. Triangles you remember – we drew some and looked around the school. Gilliam you are listening today, you tell us *(Gilliam does not have her hand up)* – triangles *(draws a triangle in the air with her hands; other children wave and make 'I am bursting to tell you' noises)* . . .
Gilliam:	*(pause)* The end of the Toblerone box?
T:	Yes, right, that is the shape. Yes. But what do we know about them? Ria?
R:	Three sides.
T:	*(not entirely satisfied)* Ye–es, three sides. Anything else?
R:	Three angles.
T:	Not you Ria, let's give everyone a chance. Tamar. On your bottom. William?
W:	Three sides and three angles, the same?
T:	OK, well, OK. Three sides and three angles, but maybe not always the same, for a triangle. Remember? OK. *(moves on to questions about a square)*

Comment

This sort of talk is a complete waste of time in terms of learning. Why is it a waste of time? The answer is not simple, but is worth teasing out, because this sort of talk is universal in classrooms. It is well meaning, and the children seem to be joining in. But it is really pointless.

To find out why it is so futile, first we can look at some of the talk tools the teacher uses:

1   A brief marker to indicate that the lesson has begun.
2   Questions.
3   Reformulations – repeating and refining children's answers to fit the story of the lesson.
4   Recapitulations – repetitions and reminders about previous learning.
5   Commands to do with behaviour.
6   Feedback on responses.

In short, the teacher orchestrates the class talk. The questions are meant to engage children by appealing to their memories and their willingness to contribute. The teacher asks five questions, all of which are uninteresting. Some children contribute to the conversation. Most do not. Those that recall the last lesson learn nothing from this conversation; those that do not, learning nothing also. This would not be a problem if this sort of talk was infrequent, but such sessions can go on for ten or 15 minutes at a time, three or four times a day. The best we can say is that a few children are using key vocabulary.

The teacher constantly uses talk to deal with behaviour, such as putting up hands to bid for turns, or to show 'listening', or not sitting nicely. Primary children are often praised for 'sitting beautifully', and really you do wonder quite why this particular skill attracts such approval. Of course it is because those who are sitting beautifully are quiet and still, making the tedious question-and-answer routine seem more fluent and important. But those who conduct a sort of personal mini-riot in the form of shuffling, playing with shoelaces, drifting off into a dream or – heaven forbid – kneeling up, know what to expect. 'On your bottoms!' I think this phrase should be banned, along with 'sitting beautifully', 'I wonder who is going to tell me . . .' and 'I should be able to see more hands than that!'

Some of the 'rules' that govern this sort of classroom talk are:

1   The teacher talks, asking 'teacher's questions' – to which she already has an answer in mind.
2   The children listen, or appear to, and speak when invited.
3   Only some ideas are acceptable, and the teacher knows which.
4   'Hands up' signals a willingness to answer (strange variations are becoming more common as teachers try to move away from 'hands up' but to be honest, 'thinking thumbs' or other signals all have the same function).
5   'Calling out' is not allowed, except sometimes when a teacher is looking for a particular response and hears it said.
6   The teacher provides no straightforward information or explanation without cross-questioning the children.

These esoteric rules, not found in any other social setting, are learned rapidly when children enter school. This class can be seen to know them quite well.

We can identify some time-wasting features of the talk:

T: Can anybody tell me what we did in Numeracy last week?

By asking the children to think back, the teacher tries to contextualise future learning. The question is a typical 'teacher's question' – that is, a question to which the teacher already knows the answer. Most ignore it. It is not interesting. The idea of guessing what is in the teacher's mind has little appeal; someone else will play the game. And last week is a very long time ago.

Blake: Traditional tales?
T: No, listen, numeracy. Numbers.

Blake offers an idea of something that happened last week – the wrong thing. The problem of defining numeracy as 'numbers' does not help children who are thinking of triangular shapes as maybe having points or lines or colours.

T: Come on, you were all there. Polly? *(Polly does not have her hand up)*
Polly: Triangles?

Teachers often choose those children not waving their hands about. This may be to check who is paying attention, to bring up short someone who is misbehaving, or sometimes to choose a child who will reliably have the right answer. Children learn to put up their hands if they don't know the answer. Some children always put up their hands; others never do.

T: Tamar sit on your bottom.

It is worryingly common to hear teachers say this to children. Why is Tamar wriggling about, or kneeling up? She is likely to be bored. What else could she be doing to learn about shapes? How long have the children been sitting on the floor? And do we think it is a good idea to comment regularly on children's bottoms in learning situations?!

Gilliam: The end of the Toblerone box?

Instead of asking Gilliam to elaborate on this useful idea, the teacher rejects it as not quite what she has in mind. The children must keep guessing what she is thinking.

> R: Three angles.
> T: Not you Ria, let's give everyone a chance.

Ria has contravened the rule that when invited, a single answer is required. To say more is tempting once you have broken the barrier and spoken, but here the teacher reminds the class that it is not only knowledge that is important, but 'giving everyone a chance'. She is assuming that her questions will engage their thinking. It has not.

> W: Three sides and three angles, the same?
> T: OK, well, OK. Three sides and three angles, but maybe not always the same,
>   for a triangle.

What does William mean by 'the same'? The teacher assumes that he thinks the angles or sides measure the same and gives him half-hearted feedback. But maybe he meant that the number, three, is the same. We will never know.

I suggest that a better start to this lesson would be for the teacher to hold up a triangle and say to the children:

> Last week we looked at triangles – here is one – it has three sides and three angles. We looked at squares and rectangles too. Think on your own or with the person next to you; what's the difference between a triangle and a square? Think what you can say that will help us all to remember.

The children can share ideas. (Astonishingly I have seen some classes do so for as little as ten seconds before being stopped.) They can then offer suggestions – and they can be asked by name, avoiding the hands-up problems – and the teacher can go on to introduce the cubes and pyramids that are the lesson focus. That did not happen for some time in the lesson transcribed. And then instead of pointing out key features (such as six faces, 12 edges, six corners) the children had to carry on guessing what the teacher wanted them to know. Such questioning is very frustrating to watch, and for children, must be endlessly tedious and hard to understand. Why do we never tell children things? I think they would like us to.

It is the questions that are the problem. Teachers' questions proliferated in an age when there was a shift from didactic teacher talk in silent rooms, to trying to involve children a little more. Now, it is almost revolutionary to suggest that a teacher should clearly explain something to children, without asking a lot of questions along the way. But the questions have become less and less useful, more and more leaden and heavy, and are now millstones hung around teachers' necks, passed on to every new generation of education students. This is how to teach – we must involve the children, and that means: ask them some questions! We must string them along, allowing them to think they are smart and know the answers! We must make them interact with us by offering some of them an occasional chance to give a one-word answer. We must never tell them anything because they really must *discover it for themselves*!

But this is not teaching. Children discover nothing by playing this guessing game. The questions are not authentic. Teachers' questions allow teachers to pull out of children words that the class needs to hear. Teachers' questions do have their uses – questions such as 'What is this called?' 'What is the difference between 12 and seven?' – will elicit answers for all to hear, and help identify those who know and those who don't. But often, episodes of interminable questions leave the class and the teacher quite baffled by one another, and do not help children to understand anything. New teachers copy those who have had years of practice at handling children this way. Children, having little choice, rapidly learn the rules. (Those who will not play along can be seen sitting around the fringes of the carpet in whole class sessions – with the Teaching Assistant, at the teacher's knee – carefully staying very quiet, or creating their own minor rumpus.) It seems that teaching and learning proceed through such conversations. But if we are honest, it does not.

Transcript 2: The Great Fire of London is an extract from a whole class session with a Year 3 class. The children were seated on a carpet and the teacher had a laptop from which she showed pictures of London on the Interactive White Board (IWB). We can consider the impact of teacher's questions on individual children in this sequence.

Transcript 2: The Great Fire of London

(Teacher puts up a slide of a London street in the 1600s)

T:	London, then, what can we see?
Children:	('houses' . . . 'the sky' . . . 'dark')
T:	Quiet please. Quiet. Hands up (hands go up) Kellen?
Kellen:	Can we see the fire?
T:	No, um, first we have to find out about London, what it was like. Take a look at the detail. Romilly?
Romilly:	Houses?
T:	Houses. What were they . . . are they like our houses? Sam?
Sam:	Yes (this is the 'wrong' answer)
T:	Oh? Really? The same –?
Sam:	. . . like, . . . um, roofs and the windows, there are windows and doors –
T:	Oh yes but, the size of them, or, how many houses in the street? Look –
Rafferty:	I know about the Great Fire of London.
T:	Just a minute, Rafferty.
Rafferty:	I went there, it started in Pudding Lane, in the bread shop, I –
T:	Oh don't tell them, they have to find it out for themselves. Now. Look again at the houses –

Comment

'What can we see?' – 'Are they like our houses'? These are dull questions. Sam guesses wrong, although his ideas are correct; the teacher agrees with him twice; but it is not what she wanted, and so the inquisition must go on. Kellen's question – 'Can we see the fire?' – is pertinent; why can't the children look at a slide or printed picture of the fire? Wouldn't that grip them? Of course, so why not? It seems to be because the session had to proceed through the ubiquitous and deadening question-and-answer routine. Giving away 'the answer' – the fire – would, like Rafferty's knowledge, stop the children somehow 'discovering' it for themselves.

Rafferty, it turns out, has been with his family to the museum in London. Interestingly the teacher stops him sharing his knowledge. She really does believe that the children will 'find out for themselves' through her questions, and this learning will somehow be more valid. But I have no doubt that to stand Rafferty up at the front and give him a few minutes to describe all he knows would be of immense benefit to the children's thinking. An expert amongst us! No weird questions to answer! Information freely given! But the teacher is very wary of this.

The idea of children *discovering things* is engrained in her approach and she believes that her questions aid this process. The questions are prompts to thinking, in a way; unfortunately their prompt value is more than cancelled out by how dreary it all is. Motivation and interest faded perceptibly as the slideshow went on. Each slide took four or five minutes, and involved more and more desperate questioning as the teacher tried to win back the children's attention. By the last slide, a picture of St Paul's, the children were shuffling and fidgeting and had to be reminded to 'sit beautifully'.

Discovery is actually impossible in some situations – one of these being sitting on a carpet with 29 classmates while looking at pictures on a screen and being asked tedious questions ('How many fields can you see? What is the river called?'). The children were finally asked to share a set of non-fiction books and find a picture of a house to draw. They squabbled over the books.

I suggest a better start to this topic would be to show a picture of the Great Fire of London and ask the children who knows anything at all about it. The children could be asked to think about why the houses burnt quite so catastrophically. As well as talking about the fire, the children could usefully discuss how best to share books, what sharing means and who is good at it, how to ask and how to offer help. Then the picture drawing could take place with the enquiry in mind, and much less arguing about resources. The fire was not mentioned again in the lesson, but the pictures were labelled *windows*, *door*, *roof* – the words Sam had used before everyone stopped listening.

The teacher is using the same talk tools as in Transcript 1 – a starting marker, teacher's questions, repetitions – but another feature of the talk is evident here. Teachers seem unwilling to tell children that an answer is wrong or inappropriate. Instead they must use a particular, rather kindly 'Are you sure?' tone of voice coupled with a suggestion that there may be something amiss – 'Um, well, let's see if anyone agrees with you . . .' or as the teacher says here, 'Really?' Children are not fooled by such evasions. Patronised in this way, they soon learn to avoid giving an answer unless they are completely certain they are right, to avoid the horrible embarrassment of a teacher saying to them, 'Mmm! That is such a good guess, but perhaps we could ask someone to help you . . .'.

I suggest that questions used to test knowledge should be answered accurately. 'Sharan, what is six multiplied by five?' 'Twenty-five.' 'We–ll, good try, but not quite . . .' is not a talk sequence that can support learning. 'Sharan, what is six multiplied by five?' 'Twenty-five.' 'No' leaves everyone in no doubt. Maybe Sharan's immortal soul would be deeply bruised by this, but I don't think so. I think it is better to be honest and clear with children. They know what 'not quite' means anyway. Sam's 'Yes' is not wrong, but does not fit the teacher's previously decided narrative, so she treats it as wrong. The teacher has in mind the idea of the children discovering that the houses were flimsier, made of wood, huddled together, and so on. But, 'Yes,' says Sam. Here is a chance to find out what the child really thinks.

'In what way?' would bring this out, followed by a suggestion to consider all the similarities and differences, particularly thinking about what creates a fire hazard.

Perhaps this is a harsh analysis. I suggest observing how colleagues, students or teachers on Teachers TV teach, with a focus on counting how many questions the teacher asks to which she already knows the answer. Some of these may have a useful function; we note that Sharan cannot multiply five by six. But many will be to do with forcing children into a ridiculous and utterly tedious guessing game, under the illusion that this is teaching.

In **Transcript 3: What seeds need**, the teacher is starting a topic on growing plants with Year 5. What learning is going on?

Transcript 3: What seeds need

T:	Right. Now. What do seeds need to grow? *(hands go up)* Alice?
Alice:	Sunlight and [. . .] water.
T:	Hmm *(sounding uncertain)* sunlight and water, you think. What else? *(fewer hands)* Bryce?
Bryce:	Earth.
Kieran:	Compost.
T:	Put your hand up. You might be chosen to talk if you put your hand up. *(Kieran puts up his hand)* Hmmm come on, someone different. Muj?
Muj:	Something to grow in.
T:	Yes something to grow in, but what else? To grow?
Chloe:	Blue pellets to keep away slugs.
T:	That's not vital. What else does it have to have? What other vital things? We've got sunlight, water and soil.
Denes:	Can worms help them grow? On my Gran's allotment, right, she has worms, they –
T:	*(dismissively)* Worms!
Denes:	*(nodding)* Yes.
Alice:	Yes in the soil, they make holes in the soil.
T:	Yes – help the soil. Absolutely. Worms. Right, now I want you to put together a role play for me . . .

Comment

The teacher had not decided whether to stick to talking about germination (seeds usually need water, air and some warmth) or to talk about plant growth (plants usually need sunlight, water, air and some warmth and usually a growing medium such as soil). She asks six teachers' questions. She accepts the children's suggestions, sunlight, water and soil – without sounding too confident about it – but has another idea in mind, and prompts the children to guess what it is. I am not sure what she wanted them to say – possibly warmth, or air. The interesting idea of slug pellets reminds Denes of soil creatures and he asks a question about worms, which is dismissed as nonsensical by the teacher but picked up by his classmate Alice. Alice's idea that worms make holes reminds the teacher that worms do help plants – which is what she asked – by aerating soil. But this is slightly too complex an idea to fit in the simpler narrative that plants need sunlight, water, soil and . . . air? Warmth?

The teacher has put herself in the position of arbiter of all knowledge, and so has to cover up the slight muddle by rapidly moving on. This cannot happen when questions are genuine and everyone is on a quest for information or understanding. Teachers do better when they make it clear what they do not know, or what is new to them, clarifying their role as part of the enquiry rather than the complete solution.

The children have no chance to share what they genuinely know or understand. It is evident that Alice seems to understand what plants require, Denes has experience of allotments, Chloe has learned about keeping slugs at bay, Kieran offers the suggestion of compost as a different medium from soil, Muj may be summing up what soil and compost are, or is aware that plants need a habitat, even if it's simply a plant pot. These ideas are not what the teacher wants. Each suggestion is taken as an end point, rather than an opener to a wider discussion.

But what is she trying to teach? The Learning Intention for this session was 'To be able to say what seeds need to grow into plants.' I suggest that it might be more productive to hand out some seeds and ask the children to tell each other everything they can think of about how to help the seed grow into a big plant. The teacher can then invite children to share what they have heard, or nominate a classmate who they think has something interesting to offer. Having established conditions for germination, and growth, the teacher can then point out or explain the difference; and then summarise the conditions as a list and move on to organising the role play.

The teacher's final words in this extract, 'for me . . .' are interesting. The teacher is not really asking for help or appealing to the children's better nature, as in 'Please make a cup of tea for me . . .'. She is casting herself as audience, judge and jury. The role plays, rather than helping children to learn, are to be 'gifts' for her. We cannot tell what the outcome will be if they don't satisfy, but the children probably know.

In **Transcript 4: Eating apples**, the teacher has 21 Year 3 children seated on the carpet. The Learning Intention is 'To use a range of strategies to subtract numbers up to 30'. This extract enables us to identify a kind of crossover talk in which teachers' questions are being phased out in favour of a more authentic sort of query.

Transcript 4: Eating apples

> T: OK, what if I have 12 apples in my bag and I get hungry and eat 4 of them. Now that's too many to use your fingers. How many left? Turn to your partners and work it out.
>
> *(children talk for about 45 seconds)*
>
> T: OK, how do you work it out? What sum do you do? *(several hands up)* Holly?
> H: Eight.
> T: Not the answer, the sum. What did you do?
> H: I worked it out [. . .] by working with Sacha, we had 12 fingers –
> T: Ah, I see. Hmm. Anyone else? What sum? Chara?
> C: We did: 12 take away two makes ten, ten take away two makes eight –
> T: Ah, very clever. Can you all see that? *(writes and says, $4 = 2 + 2$, $12 - 2 = 10$, $10 - 2 = 8$).*

T: Brilliant guys. Now who thinks . . . *(children chat and shuffle)* – I'll just wait
          a second for you to stop fidgeting. Sit on bottoms. Cross legs. Sitting still.
          Right. Who thinks . . .

Comment

The teacher made sure that the children thought about the numbers and how to manipulate
them, and asked a genuine question – 'what did you do?' She really does not know what
strategy the children used, and invites them to tell her and the class. The chance to discuss
strategies is a valuable learning opportunity. To listen to Holly, Chara and the teacher is
another chance to understand. However, the teacher had in mind a strategy she would have
preferred them not to use, and this influences her responses.

Put yourself in Holly's place, who had the sum right but whose method was evaluated as
something to be a bit ashamed of; or Chainey, who had the correct answer but wasn't invited
to speak; or Melin, who still had not solved the problem, and did not understand the written
sum on the board; or Tom, who had calculated the answer the instant the teacher provided
the numbers. What effect would this talk have on your learning?

I suggest that this teacher could helpfully start with concrete objects and show some
subtraction strategies. Abstract numbers, and the dreadful handwriting which the whiteboard seems always to generate, are not really conducive to understanding. She could stand
12 children up and have them be apples, or use big pieces of paper, or blocks. She could
show an example of separating the number four into its component twos, or show how to
count backwards in ones, twos or threes, and so on. She could explain or demonstrate
strategies which are alternatives to counting on fingers. She might then provide the
children with several puzzles to answer and give them time to talk them through. By listening
to their talk, she can choose which children will contribute to the whole class feedback.
This teacher was genuinely trying to find out what the children thought and how they
manipulated numbers. But the pace of the session was so numbingly slow that ultimately
she had to revert to the sitting-still reminders. Sometimes, why children don't actually riot
I do not know.

The teacher's talk toolkit

Teachers use talk for many reasons during a school day. They make swift decisions about
what to say and do. Their professional repertoire includes talk for learning and talk to sort
out behaviour – this is essential, but I am not concerned here with talk for giving instructions
about playtime or how to walk along the corridor. It is of course important to use talk to
ensure that children's behaviour enables everyone to learn. For the moment however, I will
defer thinking about talk for behaviour management, and simply think about talk which could
be considered as *talk for learning*.

Talk for learning

Using talk we can do the following classroom work:

1. Ask questions

Authentic, or to which we already know the answer.

2. Create a working relationship with children

Find out what children do or do not know or understand.
Check what they are interested in.
Ensure motivation and engagement with the topic in hand.
Attend to the child's emotional state.

3. Give clear explanations

Use resources to describe and demonstrate.
Tell children what they need to know.
Tell stories, read text, evaluate and analyse problems.
Model effective ways of talking and thinking.
Answer children's questions.
Instruct and check for understanding.

4. Help children to explain what they think and why

Orchestrate whole class dialogue.
Ask thought-provoking questions.
Chain ideas into a line of thinking.
Support children's elaboration of ideas.
Elicit hypothetical or uncertain ideas.
Talk through misconceptions and errors.
Help children to evaluate and analyse ideas.
Help children to synthesise new ideas.

In **Transcript 5: Iron**, the teacher is conducting a whole class plenary session with a Year 5 class who have been studying electrical conductivity through practical activity. They have just packed away the equipment. The teacher again uses *questions*, but not all teachers' questions. We can look for indicators of *creating relationships, giving explanations,* and *helping children discuss their ideas.*

Transcript 5: Iron

T:	That's really good. What, what thing would you like to go on to next, or do again, or find out about?
Matthew:	Well we just wanted to see if any other electrical conductors can be turned into magnets.
T:	Ah, that would be interesting wouldn't it? Have you got anything in mind? Could you think of anything? No? But it would be worth a go wouldn't it? Could we turn tin foil into a magnet? Um, maybe we would be able to try that next time.

Polly:	What about a coin?
T:	A coin, yes – I wonder if we could? I don't know. That would be great wouldn't it? What do you reckon, do you think we could? What do you think?
Class:	Yes
T:	What are coins made of? Hera?
Hera:	Metal . . . like . . .
T:	Can you say a bit more about what you mean – metal –
Hera:	The metal nail we had, it was iron and it lit up the bulb . . . it was a conductor –
Alex:	Cornflakes have iron.
T:	Well! Cornflakes have iron, yes, but I don't think . . . *(class laugh)*

Comment

The talk is evidence of the teacher's interest in the children's thinking. The question: 'what would you like to find out about?' is genuine. The question: 'what are coins made of?' is a teacher's question; however, Hera's brief answer is treated as just an indicator of what she might contribute. She is prompted to elaborate and responds by offering the key words, metal, iron, conductor. With no invitation, Alex makes the link between iron in this context and another everyday occurrence of the word – a mineral which features in cornflakes advertising. The teacher takes this seriously and it is the class that realises that Alex is joking. The teacher did not reprimand Polly or Alex for speaking out, or comment on other behaviour. The class was focused on the science, and 'behaving beautifully' just by doing that.

Teachers almost always have the underlying aim of encouraging children to extend their thinking; talk is the medium through which this happens, and teachers can ensure thinking goes on by asking – or helping children to ask – genuine questions. Teachers can aim to support children as they give extended answers to such real questions. The session might now take a sidestep into a discussion about the difference between iron nails and iron in cornflakes, and why we need to eat iron, and if this makes our bodies good conductors – and this would be excellent. It is important to follow these thinking trails.

Much of the teacher's input in **Transcript 5: Iron** uses talk tools to *help children discuss their ideas*:

Teacher's questions:	2	('Could we turn tin foil into a magnet?' 'What are coins made of?')
Relating:	1	('That's really good')
Explaining:	0	
Discussing children's ideas:	10	('What thing would you like to go onto next?' 'That would be interesting wouldn't it?' 'Have you got anything in mind?' 'Could you think of anything?' 'It would be worth a go wouldn't it?' 'I wonder if we could? I don't know.' 'That would be great wouldn't it?' 'What do you reckon, do you think we could?' 'What do you think?' 'Can you say a bit more about what you mean?')

In comparison we can look at the talk tools used in **Transcript 1: Triangles**:

Teacher's questions:	5	('Can anybody tell me what we did in Numeracy last week?' 'What did we do?' 'What is important about a triangle?' 'But what do we know about them?' 'Anything else?')
Relationships:	0	(not counting input on how to sit on a carpet)
Explaining:	3	('Numeracy. Numbers: Shape is what we were doing, 2-D shapes: Three sides and three angles')
Discussing children's ideas:	0	

Perhaps we can see from this simple analysis why I said that I think such talk is a complete waste of time. The teacher does not know how the children are feeling, and does not make sure that they are motivated or interested. She tells them three things which most of them knew already. This minimal information is given in a muddled way, mixed in with an increasingly anxious teacher's questions to try to make the children think – or at least speak. Little learning happens.

In **Transcript 6: Function machine**, a Year 4 teacher is at the whiteboard. She is showing the class how to use an electronic maths game, in which the task is to find out what *function* (+, −, × or ÷) the machine carries out on numbers entered, by looking at the output provided. What learning goes on?

Transcript 6: Function machine

T:	OK. I'm going to put a number in – (*looks at class quizzically*)
Louis:	One thousand!
T:	OK . . . Louis immediately said one thousand. Is that a good number to put in?
Kyle:	No.
T:	You're shaking your head. Why do you think it's not? Shall we come back to you? You've got an idea but you can't explain it? OK, Louis had one thousand. Anybody think yes or no to that idea? David?
David:	Start off with an easier number.
T:	Start off with an easier number. By an easier number what kind of number do you mean?
David:	Um, something like, lower, five.
T:	Fine. A smaller number, a lower number, yes. Louis can you see that point of view?
Louis:	Yes.
T:	If we put in a thousand we could end up with a huge number. If we put in five do you think it will be easier to work out what the machine has done?
Class:	Yes.
T:	Everyone agree?
Class:	Yes.
T:	OK, I'm going to type in five.

Comment

The teacher is listening to the children, and using their ideas. She asks for ideas and gives children the opportunity to explain their thinking. She explains the 'point of view' that a lower number will make things easier. The children are familiar with this phrase – they know that suggestions can be challenged, and a range of points of view will be considered. She checks that the first child sees why his suggestion might make things difficult. She also checks that the class agree with the new suggestion before using it. You could fault the teacher because she is a little directive; but classroom talk is never perfect, and we can see that she is talking to the children the way she would like them to talk to one another. Chapter 3 explains how to teach children to engage one another in this sort of exploratory talk.

Conclusions

If we assume that teachers know things and children need to be taught them, then it should be children who ask the questions. But in primary classrooms, this does not often happen. A set curriculum, rigid and incomprehensible Learning Intentions, rapid and meaningless changes between subjects throughout the day, and no idea of any overall personal aim for education, mean that children in classrooms are passive. They have learned how to sit beautifully, how to make a good guess, and how to keep a low profile.

Heartbreakingly, this is not what primary teachers want. Teachers know that children are lively-minded, creative creatures with their own agendas for learning. But teachers under the baleful eye of the always-impending Ofsted inspection, like a permanent CCTV camera in the mind, must get through curricula, jump between subjects, make children achieve targets, follow rigid routines, go with the precepts of ever-changing initiatives and strategies, 'drive up standards', use the limited software provided with the whiteboard – indeed, there is little time to do anything else if the individualised assessment documents are to be completed – they must forget their vocation. They must avoid too much discussion, because it's time consuming. They must avoid too close a relationship with the children, because this, too, is time consuming. They must not explain anything, because children must find out for themselves. So it is that we arrive at the current position. On most mornings, you can go into school and see up to 30 children seated on a carpet, with a teacher valiantly trying to get them to answer inane questions, while time flows away. It is a tribute to both teachers and children that they work so hard at it all and still remain friendly and relatively calm. I think if the current situation had been imposed overnight, say in 1995, there would have been uproar. But it has evolved slowly and insidiously, eroding creativity, confidence, interest, individuality, flair, learning and teaching.

Fortunately, somehow, many, many teachers manage to keep coming up with gripping things to do and fascinating ideas; they help children to see the bigger picture, get them thinking, and subvert the rigid Learning Intentions with their enthusiasm. They find out how children are feeling and what they want to know and do. They put children's time to good use in meaningful activity and interesting quests. And funnily enough, their classes do very well when faced with tests.

Chapter 2

ON THE CARPET

Teacher–pupil dialogue [. . .] compels most of the class to listen in silence.

(Barnes, 1992: 78)

The question-and-answer method of control must in the long run devalue – in the pupils' eyes as much as the teacher's – the pupils' capacity for taking a responsible part in learning.

(Barnes, 1992: 176)

This chapter looks at the talk we use during whole class lesson introductions. Since introductions often take place with children gathered on the carpet, it is worth including this particular context for learning in an analysis of what makes our talk with children more, or less, effective. In any lesson introduction, many things are happening at once. We need to find out what children already know, help them to share their ideas, and give them new information and things to think about. Meanwhile we have to capture everyone's attention and make sure that we explain what will happen once the introduction is over.

How can we help children to get the best out of lesson introductions? One way is to teach children to understand what is happening in an introduction, and to clarify for them the part they can play.

Preparing children to take part in whole class discussion

Children come into class immersed in the intricacies and excitements of their own lives. As teachers, we must ask them to put aside all this for a little while, and attend to Learning Intentions which we know will benefit them in the long run. To get the best out of lesson introductions, children need to focus their attention, and stay focused. This requires a great deal of motivation, and the ability to switch from individual concerns to listening and responding to others. Knowing why they must do so can help. Recognising the signals – that this is 'one of those whole-class times' – comes easily to some children. For others, personal interests and concerns dominate and cannot be left till later. As adults, we can recognise this problem. If we think of how staff meetings begin, there is often a flurry of personal conversation and exchange of ideas before people settle down. Social talk is extremely important. But then we defer our 'real' lives for a while in the interests of sorting out management details or learning of new strategies or ideas – though we might admit that sometimes thoughts wander, and large group meetings provide a chance to write a 'to do' list or doodle some crucial thought that has just come to mind.

For a child, inattention leads to what might be thought of as inappropriate behaviour; the chance to chatter, fiddle with shoes, twiddle with someone else's hair, or try to make your friend laugh. We can help children by teaching them to attend to what they hear and relate it to their own thinking.

Children ready to work with the whole class are:

- familiar with the Learning Intentions
- ready to listen to their teacher and one another
- willing to contribute their own ideas
- able to articulate their thinking and hold ideas in mind while others are talking
- able to ask clear questions
- able to challenge what they hear
- used to giving reasons for ideas
- able to change their minds – to think flexibly
- motivated and wish to take part.

In summary, children need to know that a dialogue is expected and that they should be part of it. Amazingly, most children from Reception onwards do seem to know this; they often sit quietly and attend during whole class sessions. It's very impressive. But all children need a clear understanding of *why* whole class sessions take place – what's in it for them – and how to take part fully.

On the carpet

'On the carpet' is where British primary school children may spend a surprisingly high proportion of their school day. Carpet sessions can really benefit learning. But they can also seem interminable if not well managed. Asked why they like to talk to children seated on a carpet, teachers often mention creating a collaborative atmosphere; children seated in a group do look as if they are a tight-knit mini-community. But this can be an illusion. In reality they may be uncomfortable, irritable and just not listening. Collected from teachers, the following 'pointers' can help to make sure that every child benefits from carpet sessions.

Pointers for effective carpet sessions

Learning Intentions

Have these and other information already written or displayed. It is not necessary for children to copy Learning Intentions down. Given that they have not yet learnt what is intended, they may not know what they are writing.

Starting the day

Is the carpet really the best place for children while you take the register: could they be at tables with a quiet task to think about?

Questions

Plan and use *authentic* questions to:

- engage interest and focus attention
- guide a discussion
- encourage shared understanding
- generate common knowledge
- prompt suggestions.

Try to minimise 'teachers' questions' – that is, questions to which you already know the answer:

'What colour tummies do robins have? What is dangerous about scissors? Where do snails live?'

Children's responses are dulled by awareness that they must guess the answer you have in mind. They may simply leave this task to others. We can ask real questions that invite opinions, information, previous understanding from lessons, and children's own ideas based on their everyday experiences.

'What do you know about robins? What do you think is a safe way to use scissors? When did you last see a snail?'

Instructions

Use clear instructions, rather than questions, to explain Learning Intentions, provide information and detail activities. Questioning can reduce the coherence of your input. Use brief questions to check for understanding. Explain things you want the children to understand.

Hands up

Asking for 'hands up' favours the confident, the articulate and those who have learned how to join in. But it is the other children who need the chance to talk to the entire class. 'Hands up' may not always be the most effective way to include children in discussion. It's impossible to choose all those who wish to talk. Quieter children can evade notice. Stopping children calling out becomes the focus for the discussion. Try some other ways.

Ask children to turn to their neighbours. Decide who will be 'person A' and who will be 'person B'. Ask As to talk to Bs for one minute, then swap. Then you can ask any child by name for either their idea or their partner's idea. This avoids children having to bid for attention by putting up hands. Or, start by asking children not to put hands up. Ask them to remember not to speak until invited. Then:

- Ask a particular child for their response: after answering they then 'pass it on' to a child of their choice.

- Explain that you are going to choose, and everyone must be prepared to contribute.
- Ask five children to stand at the front. As you ask questions, they choose which of their classmates will answer, then go to sit down. Select another five 'volunteers'.
- Tell children in advance which individuals or group will be asked to speak. That way you can ensure a balance, though it does reduce spontaneity.
- Ask for contributions from a mix of those who usually speak and those less confident.
- Ask children to share what they think with one another rather than the whole class.
- Address questions to children in the order they are seated. Tell them that you are going to do this, and that they can nod or shake their heads to show whether they wish to answer.
- Ask children to collect a small sticker to wear as they move onto the carpet. Wearing this shows that they would like to speak in the class discussion. Have a class list on which children put their stickers at the end of sessions to build up a tally. Decide who needs support in whole class discussions.

Stop while you're winning

It's fascinating talking with children and easy to forget the time. There is usually a lot to get through so it's crucial to have resources prepared, to provide straightforward information, and to keep questions focused. Children need a change of pace, a chance to move, talk to one another or start an activity. Your impact is lessened as they gradually switch off from your voice. You also need to take a break from leading the class from the front. Supporting individuals and groups is just as demanding, but in a different way. After 15–20 minutes, send your class from the carpet feeling enthusiastic, having had a good experience, and looking forward to coming back for more.

Managing transitions

Ask the class to get started at their tables.

- Keep just the children you need to talk to a little longer.
- Ask the class to spend a few minutes telling each other what they are about to do, why, and how.
- Take a few moments to work through some stretching and flexing exercises to energise children after sitting.
- Give children time to play with new equipment for a few minutes before the 'work' starts. Magnets, calculators, water, new pencils – all such fascinating things need to be inspected and mulled over before the child can begin to use them in accordance with our Learning Intentions.

Carpet privileges

Organise a rota of groups to work on the carpet during appropriate activities. Cushions, laptops, different pens, whiteboards or clipboards, special resources, can make things interesting and help motivation.

Making the most of the carpet

Have a day of the week when the carpet is not used for whole class work. Groups or individuals can use the carpet for reading, sharing, discussing, planning, spreading out resources, etc. This will help maintain the novelty value and promote the idea of the carpet as a place for collaborative learning. Use the carpet for singing, clapping games, finger puppet shows, drama, role play, display and looking at a new resource a group at a time. Provide big books in which children can record ideas on a topic or curriculum theme, or have a special page each. Children can visit the carpet and add a picture or text during group work.

Find out what the children think

What do your class think about their time on the carpet? Ask them! You could try a questionnaire; use or adapt the format provided here. You could provide multi-choice answers: ask the children to type their answers; or ask your Teaching Assistant to interview children. It can be really informative to discover children's opinions. They make creative and useful suggestions for effective use of carpet time and like to know that you value their ideas.

Working on the carpet – questionnaire

In what ways do we learn things when sitting all together on the carpet?

Do you enjoy working on the carpet?   Why/Why not?

I like it on the carpet when   because

I don't like it when   because

I like to sit near   because

I think it would be better working on the carpet if
because

I think the carpet should be used for
because

I think the carpet shouldn't be used for
because

Resources

Pass round concrete resources such as objects, pictures, etc., to make key points and ensure that the introduction is not too abstract.

Making Learning Intentions clear

Learning Intentions, shared with the class, help children to understand what they are doing and why. They can also raise children's awareness of the importance of working together in whole class sessions. However, copying a Learning Intention which is a meaningless list of unfamiliar words is a very disheartening way to start a lesson. By the nature of things, Learning Intentions state what children do not know. So, it is crucial to phrase Learning Intentions as brief, interesting statements which are completely comprehensible to the learner.

A Year 6 class I visited were carefully writing the literacy Learning Intention: 'To understand how writers use different structures to create coherence and impact'. A brief survey of the class indicated that a significant majority of the children were copying this without a jot of understanding. Similarly, a Year 3 Numeracy class were laboriously writing: 'To interpret drawings of shapes and use reflective symmetry to draw and complete shapes'.

It is evident that if the child is to find motivation in knowing what they are doing, they have to understand the language in which ideas are expressed. It is not 'dumbing down' to clarify ideas by re-phrasing them. Year 6 could be studying 'Different writers, different ways of saying things, different effects on the reader' – no need to write that down; and the Year 3 class could be thinking about 'To understand how shapes can be drawn' – again, why write it? Ideas about reflective symmetry could be recorded in the plenary, once the learning about it has happened.

The teachers both told me that using Learning Intentions straight from the National Strategies web pages helped them to mark children's work and see what topics had been covered. They said that parents liked it. I imagine they meant that parents might feel their child had reached a higher plane of understanding, having written such obscure things; but of course copying is not *knowing*. Learning Intentions must be intelligible and should support learning, not assessment. And what will the child learn from writing the Learning Intention down? Maybe their time can be better spent doing some of the learning intended.

Talking with children during lesson conclusions

How can children continue to benefit from talk for learning as the lesson finishes? Children may have nearly exhausted their enthusiasm; they may not feel like re-stating things already said, or listening to what others have found out. But a lesson without an effective closing plenary misses chances to consolidate what has happened, to end positively, providing conclusions and establishing new questions. It's best not to introduce new ideas at this stage. Using the Learning Intentions and success criteria, we can ask questions which allow the children to share their ideas, reflect on their learning and on how they learned:

'What did you find useful about the reading/writing/drawing/ICT work/discussion? Who helped someone else to understand something? How did you help someone else? What did you learn . . . how did you learn it? Can anyone explain this point for us now?'

Decide with the class what might be a focus for further learning in the same area and ask children to suggest how the session's learning might be used in other contexts.

Teachers have contributed the following suggestions for effective lesson conclusions.

Closing plenary discussions

- Leave enough time to talk and listen. Keep it brief and focused.
- Children should know that their ideas and efforts will be treated with interest.
- Create an atmosphere in which progress and learning are whole class ventures – success for individuals depends on success for all.
- Teach children to ask questions, provide explanations which follow on from one another, and elaborate.
- Ask a child to say how their idea links to what they have just heard.
- During group work, prepare for the closing plenary by asking individuals or groups to be ready to present their ideas, work or questions to the class. This can make subsequent carpet time more focused and involving. Ask children to present their work by name.
- Consider whether it's best to move to the carpet or stay at tables.

Teacher's talk and children's behaviour

In our professional role, we are allocated classes of disparate, lively-minded individuals, and required to ensure that they behave in ways that allow everyone to learn. Teachers make good use of talk to marshal and order their classes, to remind children of agreed rules, and to reinforce good behaviour with positive comments. 'Behaviour for learning' does not happen all at once on the first day of term, but is a slow, patient, cumulative process. A teacher's use of their voice for discipline, structure, organisation and to remind children of expectations for behaviour is extremely important. Talking to children about their behaviour is immediate, responsive and can convey tolerance and understanding as well as firmness. It's part of the job. The problem is that it is sometimes really difficult to slip between using talk to manage behaviour, and using spoken language for learning.

To evaluate how much of your time is spent on using talk to manage behaviour, ask your Teaching Assistant to keep a tally of the *purpose* of your talk for a carpet session, a whole lesson or a day. If talk to manage behaviour or classroom procedures is really what you are spending most of your time on, then it's time to review what is happening and sort things out with your class. Take a day off the curriculum and teach them about talk for learning. Most of your talk with children ought to be to do with their learning or their personal concerns – and they should know that. In fact they probably do. But 'getting teacher going' sometimes gives many of the class the chance to sit back and do nothing while you waste your breath on explaining things they already know, such as how they are expected to behave and why.

Helping classmates to learn

Transcript 7: Who's helped you learn? is an extract from a discussion between a Year 5 teacher and her class after a practical session. It shows how a class who are used to considering their classmates as a resource can identify who has helped them to learn, and how. The children are aware of the importance of talk and the public nature of the positive feedback helps to generate a truly collaborative working atmosphere. 'Who has helped you to learn?' is a useful talk tool.

Transcript 7: Who's helped you learn?

T: Um now, can anybody just say if you think anybody here, um, one of your classmates, has helped you to learn anything today? Who's helped you learn, Bobby?

Bobby: Um – Abi's helped me, because when we started um, I forgot what a parallel circuit was, and then Abi – um – connected some wire into that, and then it just sprang to mind. And if Abi hadn't had done that then I just, like this whole – this bit of the lesson would just have gone out the window.

T: But it made sense because Abi helped you? You actually enjoyed electricity today haven't you?

Bobby: Yes we've got four bulbs connected up now.

T: Are you going to be an electrician when you grow up and you're dead keen aren't you Bobby now? I've got a convert over here and it's brilliant. Jim?

Jim: I think Ethan helped me today, because – um – I didn't really understand the first question. Like make a series circuit with two bulbs, and it was a bit confusing because, and, like we were talking about that and then he just did it, and so then he explained to me.

T: So he showed you and explained to you? That's helpful isn't it? Well done Jim. Willa?

Willa: Lucy helped me on the first one, I didn't understand, and then – um – Lucy like showed me how to like make a circuit, otherwise I would have got all the things wrong but Lucy helped to explain it to me.

T: Well done Lucy, it's always good to have Lucy in the group I always find, always useful.

Conclusions

Whole class teaching is a terrific opportunity to talk with children, finding out what they think and know, providing information and instructions, and generating the motivation for children to undertake group or individual work. Talking with a class of 30 or so children can be a heady experience, as ideas and interests are aired, knowledge shared and questions raised. Some of the most productive times teachers have with children are during such sessions. Children like to share what they think, and we like to hear what they have to say. On-the-carpet sessions can create a collaborative atmosphere and can help the class to learn as a group, to have joint experiences which all can draw on later.

But having achieved quiet, it is very easy to keep children together for rather too long. It is quite difficult for teachers to discern exactly who is learning whilst managing the conversation and behaviour of so many. It is worth analysing how and when the carpet is used, thinking about who is talking and who is not so forthcoming, and why; and finding out if children are aware that the discussions we have with them are 'work' – and as such, crucial for developing thinking. Children need to take responsibility for their own learning and that of their classmates by joining in with whole-class talk. Knowing how to do so is not a natural skill, but can be taught and fostered in any child.

Lesson introductions can set up the right conditions to support learning. If we can ensure that children are engaged with the topic under discussion, we can create an atmosphere of confidence and trust in which children can admit uncertainty and share misconceptions. New learning happens as children listen to fresh ideas and have the chance to match these against their current thinking. Listening to group work can help you to determine who will contribute to the lesson conclusion. Discussion as a lesson ends can provide opportunities for sharing learning amongst children, as well as raising further questions. At all stages of the lesson, the importance of talk for learning should be made explicit. This can help children to realise that talk has the same high status as reading and writing in the classroom.

Chapter 3

GROUND RULES FOR EXPLORATORY TALK

This chapter will consider the all-important talk that happens when we ask children to work together as a group. It is at these times that powerful insights can be shared and real learning can take place. That is the ideal. In practice, children in groups often resort to social chat, carrying out activities mechanically, with their minds disengaged. Little is gained but the most superficial of outcomes. Worse, children 'fall out' or take the chance to needle or ignore one another. Fortunately it is entirely possible to teach children *how* to talk to one another when asked to discuss things with a group. Not only that, they can learn *why* such talk is crucial, and so discover the motivation and develop the skills to take part in genuine discussions. Learning how to discuss things has profound outcomes for learning across the curriculum and for children's development as both team workers and independent-minded individuals.

Direct teaching of exploratory talk

The success of everyday, talk-based activities is heavily dependent on children under-standing what we mean when we ask them to talk about their work with their classmates, and share their thinking with the whole class. It is essential when children are directly taught that everyone benefits if learning goes on 'aloud' – that thinking is shared in a way everyone can access.

The next section offers a structure for teaching such awareness and the talk skills children need. These skills are nothing to do with accents, dialects or home languages, which are all unique attributes of children's talk which should be fostered and valued. But children need to know what sort of talk creates a reasoned discussion, and how and why they can take part in such events. If they do not learn this at school, they may never learn. It's a bit like the 7 times table in a way. You may never come across it at home, but if you learn it in school, you have it in mind for good. It's a tool which can be usefully applied to various problems throughout life. Of course, learning how to take part in a reasoned discussion – that is, to use exploratory talk – is massively more useful than learning the 7 times table! (Discuss!)

Suggestions for teaching and learning exploratory talk

1. Awareness of talk for learning

Find out what your children think about whole class talk, talk in groups, talk with a partner, pair-and-share, talk in assembly and so on. Why do they think we ask them to talk sometimes, and ask them not to, at other times? Who do they think is good to talk to? Who listens well? Can they think of examples when a friend has taught them something or suggested a good idea? Can they think of times when it is helpful to work quietly alone? You will already know who likes contributing to whole class discussions and who prefers not to. Try to find out why. It's also interesting to find out what children think about sharing ideas: do they see it as 'cheating'? Are they hampered by the belief that if they share what they know, it means that they, personally, will be less likely to shine? Use a whole class discussion about a curriculum area as an example. Show how contributions have helped everyone to move on a bit in their thinking.

In summary we need to find out if individuals, and the class as a unit, understand *why* and *how* to take part effectively in whole class discussions. If they don't, they need explicit instruction, perhaps one-to-one, perhaps in a small group where you can model the relevant speaking and listening behaviour, vocabulary and positive outcomes.

2. *Asking and answering questions*

Little children ask lots of questions, but may stop doing so in class, although it's hard to believe they become less curious. We need to foster a question-friendly environment in which children's questions are answered directly, not with another question; and in which many teachers' questions are genuine, not designed to call forth a particular fact.

Children can be taught how and why to keep asking questions. They can use a thesaurus to find lots of words and phrases which are question-openers, and practice using them to devise questions for research or investigation in any subject. There can be a weekly 'question starter' which is used frequently so that it becomes common currency. ('What if? How can we? What do you think? Why?')

Topics can start with a chance to suggest questions. For example, showing a picture of Mount Vesuvius on the IWB: ('We are going to think about volcanoes. What are your starting questions? What do you want to know or understand?')

3. *Getting children into groups*

Three children is best; then there will be a range of opinions but not too many. Mixed ability is best; someone can always read and write if needed, and everyone has a chance to offer more subtle competences such as good general knowledge, ability to oil the wheels socially, being a good listener, knowing how to conduct a discussion. A mix of boys and girls is best, but a group of two boys and a girl has very different dynamics than two girls and a boy. You will know your own class best and can put together working groups which take account of personalities and preferences. It has to be said that some children may not take well to working with those they usually choose not to associate with. We cannot pretend that this is not so, but we can ensure that every child understands that talk groups are very special, not negotiable, and that each member has an equal contribution to offer. Understanding this takes time and discussion.

Some groups gel immediately, some take longer, and some never do. It is worth persisting with your original grouping. Resist entreaties for change for at least five talk group sessions.

Changing one group is the thin end of the wedge and will have repercussions . . . children are quick to interpret flexibility on your part as some sort of weakness! Stick to your original groups until you decide that children have the skills and awareness to talk to anyone in the class. Discuss this with them and praise collaborative achievement extravagantly in the early stages. Make sure that there is time after discussion sessions to talk about any difficulties groups have had, and to enable the class to make suggestions.

Some children simply cannot work in a group. They are best as observers, moving from group to group to collect ideas, to experience good models for listening and sharing reasons, and to report back on the quality of talk during the plenary. Listening to effective talk is one way of learning how to do it. Some children have years of catching up to do in terms of talk skills, and much inner disturbance to overcome if they are to get the best out of their own mind and the minds of others. We can sympathise with this without comment, and we can prevent children who cannot discuss ideas spreading their disturbance to others. It is easy for that to happen. It takes effort and commitment from the class to do the opposite, which is to help children who cannot articulate ideas and reasons to learn how to do so.

Teaching Assistants are brilliant at supporting children's attempts to join in. It's a really complex task, because 'joining in' may mean just listening, or having your idea challenged and amended – hard things to do for any child. Children learning discussion skills really need a chance to see what's in it for them – which can only happen if they are part of the talk. It's a 'Catch 22' for children with poor talk skills. They can't take part in discussion; if they try to, it tends to all fall apart. If they don't try to, they will never know how to negotiate their ideas or understand the ideas of others. In class we must cut through the problems and get them started on thinking aloud with others, reasoning, listening, elaborating and negotiating compromise, if not agreement.

4. Taking part in exploratory talk

Exploratory talk is a kind of talk that is essential for educational success. But children may not hear much of it in their out-of-school lives. These are its characteristics:

* every child contributes and asks others to contribute
* ideas are treated with respect and considered carefully
* reasons are given
* everyone listens attentively and is focused on the task
* there are hesitant suggestions and people can change their minds
* everyone is expected to elaborate on ideas
* ideas link to what has been said before
* the group tries to negotiate an agreement.

Children need to be taught about exploratory talk, which involves a sequence of lessons in which the Learning Intentions are to do with one aspect of exploratory talk (above) at a time. They need practice, reinforcement, discussion about progress, and chances to work in groups during which they use and begin to appreciate the value of exploratory talk. The value of exploratory talk is that it is inclusive, rational, measured, thoughtful and focused. It enables all group members to think through their own ideas and those of others in a friendly forum; children can take risks, expressing tentative ideas, and can hear and consider new possibilities. Ideas can be sounded out. Children need chances to experience this sort of talk. Their use of it is consolidated by practice and the chance to discuss the difference between exploratory talk and other sorts of talk they encounter in and out of school.

5. Creating ground rules for exploratory talk

Ask children to suggest their ideas about group work. It is helpful for children to reflect on what can go wrong in a group and say what they will do about it. They must be encouraged to remember that *their group* will benefit from discussing things rationally. Use the Talking Points (see Chapter 5) provided below. Ask groups to discuss the Talking Points. After time for talk, organise a whole class discussion in which you and the class link suggestions, ask others to agree or disagree and say why, and come to an agreement.

Talking Points – group discussion: what are the problems?

Are these ideas true or false?

If things are going wrong with the group, we should give up and tell the teacher.
We can think what to say to make a discussion go well.
It is not possible to find out what other people are thinking.
If someone doesn't want to talk we should leave them out.
It is wrong to change your mind.
If you can't get a word in, start shouting.
If you know something about the topic, it's best to keep it to yourself.
It is reasonable to get angry if the group disagrees with your idea.
You have to know exactly what you are going to say before you start saying it.
If someone wants to go on about their idea, explaining it in detail, you can ask them
      to cut it short.
If people talk about things that are not to do with the topic, it will be more fun.

After this preparation, ask groups to work together to create five or six 'rules' which will help everyone to discuss things using exploratory talk. You might want to provide categories for the rules:

*   Respecting and including everyone.
*   Giving reasons for ideas.
*   Listening and thinking.
*   Encouraging others to make suggestions and explain ideas.
*   Trying to reach agreement.

Once groups have had a chance to think and talk, collect the ideas. Synthesise a set of class ideas. Share this with the class and ask for their agreement.

Explain that these *ground rules for exploratory talk* are what will ensure that group work is effective and interesting for everyone. Revise and apply the rules constantly; remind children frequently; ask for examples of exploratory talk in your plenary sessions. Ask children to take a copy home and discuss the ideas with parents. Keep the rules visible and alive in the classroom until children are so familiar with them that exploratory talk becomes common. This can take weeks or longer, but is well worth your persistence. Knowing how to take part in a discussion is not a topic to be dipped into and then left; it's a crucial life skill which should be thoroughly taught and learned.

Example: Year 3 ground rules for talk

We are going to talk and listen in turns.
Everyone will say what they know and what they think.
We will ask, 'why?'
We are going to try to decide together.

---

6. Discussion activities

If a task or problem is too easy, the group have nothing to talk about and just do it with no discussion. If the task is too difficult, the children either fall out with one another, or in effect 'fall out with the task'. Either way, there is no exploratory talk, and no learning. The level of challenge of activities has to be carefully matched to the children's capabilities. Fortunately, teachers tend to have this knowledge about each child in their class; this is their professional expertise, enabling them to identify appropriate discussion points.

Every child's voice

Some children have the confidence to voice their ideas and negotiate with others through talk. What we want is to help every child to see how to join those who 'can', through augmenting their speaking and listening skills, giving them confidence and practice, and valuing their voice. For some children, the classroom may be the only place where such basic, profoundly important social tuition goes on. For those already adept in oral communication, a talk-focused classroom provides just the right environment to use and apply their social and collaborative skills. Without a certain critical mass of others who also 'can', their competence may go to waste. Children are like adults (unsurprisingly!) in that when things get tricky, they will take the easy option. So, if the classroom generally operates through *guess the answer* questioning, *sit down and get on with it quietly* work, and *keep what you know to yourself for fear of being labelled a boffin* interactions, the sensible child will keep their head down and adopt the class style. They will coast. Indeed it is social suicide to do anything else.

The less articulate child will muddle along, often devising the most astonishing strategies to cope with their bafflement and inability to join in, just as they do to cover up lack of reading skills. Some of these strategies may be subtle, but others will involve disruption, distress and a real interference with their own learning and that of others. A cycle of 'unacceptable behaviour' begins, maybe in the Reception class, or horrifyingly, even earlier. Children unable to express their emotions, ideas, thoughts or questions through talk almost have to resort to more physical ways of making their presence felt. Or they just withdraw, which is possibly even worse than creating a rumpus, given that it may be only those who 'squeak' that attract enough attention to get help. Teaching speaking and listening, raising awareness, getting the whole class to see their importance to one another, giving children a voice and listening to it, and offering them insights into how they learn, is the essence of education.

Making a group decision

Transcript 8: Group decision is an extract from a discussion in which a Year 5 class set about considering the Learning Intention 'To be able to agree on a group answer'. It's interesting to think about the teacher's use of language.

Transcript 8: Group decision

T:	I think our Learning Intention for this bit of the lesson, is to make sure that you agree on your group answer. So you might have different opinions but your focus for this session is to make sure that you're going to agree with the other people in your group. So there's a problem there, because what happens if you don't agree with them – are you just going to get up and leave the room or tell them they're rubbish? Ben what would you do?
Ben:	Um – give them reasons why that, why you think that's the answer.
T:	So you could give them a good reason, and then what if they thought your reasons weren't good reasons, what could they do?
Ben:	They could give some of their own reasons or –
T:	And they know you'd be happy to listen don't they? So they've got the chance to give you their reasons in return. Thank you, that's a help. What were you going to say Clarrie?
Clarrie:	Take it in turns to say your ideas and you can decide which was the best one.
T:	So taking turns, so everybody's heard everything, and then go with all those ideas and work out what's the best. That that sounds a good strategy as well doesn't it? Euan?
Euan:	You could always compromise.
T:	What does that mean? *(child doesn't reply)* I think you're right – give us an example?
Euan:	Well you could gather up all the ideas of the group, and then work out the points of it and try and come up with a good answer for it. And then you, once you've got your answer you actually look back at the question and see if it's a sensible answer for the question, because sometimes the answer wanders off to something stupid.
T:	That's a good point isn't it? You can lose your focus and wander off with something that's interesting – it might not be stupid but maybe not relevant. Good point. Rowan?
Rowan:	You could decide on, on a neutral answer which is one that can go either way.
T:	OK so you can come up with something that takes everybody's opinions and gives you – I like your word neutral, helpful sometimes. Fletcher?

Fletcher: Well instead of causing an argument, if two people say it, it wins, there's more answers to the 'yes' than 'no'. And if, if two of you aren't sure you put down not sure.

T: Right OK, so you could make sure that the majority of people said what they thought, but keep a note that other people thought differently. Great, well I'm going to ask you to talk about these questions in the way you just described, to come up with a group answer.

Comment

We can see the teacher using exploratory talk to teach children how to do the same: she provides a good model for the children to follow.

Conclusions

Teachers can offer children direct instruction so that they gain understanding of how and why to use exploratory talk – how to discuss things, giving reasons. With this capability, the child can take on curriculum learning, making decisions based on reasoned choices. This is an important life skill, a way in to understanding themselves and others. Perhaps you can see this happening in schools any day. But you can also see some children lost and failing; direct teaching of talk skills and understanding can help to bring them in.

Chapter 4

SPEAKING AND LISTENING FOR READING AND WRITING

One in five people in the UK struggles to read and write. Poor skills compromise the health, confidence, happiness and employability of individuals and have a negative impact on our national economy.

(The Literacy Trust)

Talk supports reading and writing

Maybe there will never be a time when everyone can read and write – there never has been so far. But it is a good aim. Encouraging children's developing literacy is rightly a primary aim in classrooms. An inability to talk with others is a real deprivation. It deprives children of one important way of learning, and of ways to communicate with others in profoundly important everyday conversations. So, while the struggle towards reading and writing goes on, we really have to do our utmost to help children develop effective ways to communicate through talk.

I regularly observe children faced with 'Literacy' Learning Intentions such as:

'To understand the purpose of instructional texts.'
'To expand vocabulary of time words and imperative verbs.'
'To employ polysyllabic adjectives to enhance descriptive text.'

How pointless. No child wants to know the features of instructional texts, or any other of the precepts taught as 'Literacy'. But they might want to write a plan in which a list of clear instructions would help; they might want to know what sort of words would help them to express their ideas in a story, poem, web page or song. 'Explore how different texts appeal to readers using varied sentence structures and descriptive language'. Really, is that even possible? Why not write a story ending, discussing how it might be made more descriptive? Or talk about how different sorts of sentences might have the effect you intended?

In this chapter, stories are used as a focus for group discussion. Reading and writing activities are based on the children's talk. The ideas mentioned here can be used with other stories, with poems, art works, electronic text, music: and with non-fiction texts in humanities, science and across the curriculum.

The stories providing contexts for talk-based literacy are:

1. *Jorian the Unimouse* – Years 3 and 4. *Jorian the Unimouse* opens in a tree house as the woodland creatures face the aftermath of a storm.

2. *Onyx Quest* – Years 5 and 6. The children in *Onyx Quest* are threatened with the loss of the family's cat under dreadful circumstances.

You can read the story aloud to the class, or ask an older, fluent reader to record a reading. You can provide 'props' in the shape of models or pictures of the characters or the settings. Children may benefit from having their own copy of the story.

Electronic versions of text, suggested endings, and activities are available on the Thinking Together website: please see Websites at the end of this book.

Jorian The Unimouse

In the night, a huge storm flashed and raged at the windows. By morning, the paths were littered with leaves and twigs, and no lights were working in Oak Tree House. Everywhere was cold and shadowy. It was obvious that someone had to go for help.

'Go and fetch Sparky Wiremouse,' said Woody. 'We'll find candles.'

Cressy and Axel crept outside into the darkness, and set off through the wood, hopping over puddles full of leaves and sky. By the field gate, a whole tree was down, lying like a giant on the ground.

'I'm glad that wasn't our house,' said Axel.

Through the darkest bit of the wood they went, where the black pine trees grew with their spiky year-round leaves.

'What's that?' said Cressy. 'Something shiny on the ground . . .'

It was a mouse, almost as still as the fallen tree. A little warily, Axel knelt down. The mouse stirred as Cressy offered her water bottle.

'Hmmmm,' he said. His wings, stretched thin like a bat's, were torn; on his forehead was a silver spike like a little needle. It was a Unimouse, bruised and crumpled by the storm. The sparkles on his cloak glinted through smears of mud. His back-pack was the only thing that seemed to be in one piece. He sat up, confused and dizzy. He had banged his head and hurt his ears.

'Oh! My lucky day!' he said. 'You're not supposed to be able to see me. I'd better get going.' He tried to stand up but immediately fell over. He obviously couldn't fly at all.

'Well we definitely can see you,' said Cressy. 'You'd better come home with us till you can fly. Or you might get eaten by the fox . . . that's much worse for you than being seen.'

At the mention of the fox, all three went perfectly still . . . except that their eyes, ears and noses checked. . . . no. No fox. Between them, Cressy and Axel helped the Unimouse up and pushed, lifted and cajoled him back

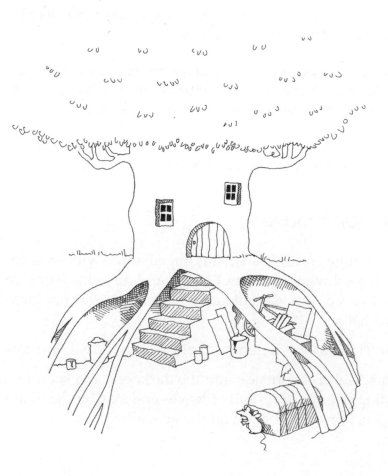

to Oak Tree House, glad now of the gloomy morning. He was still fretting about being seen.

'You can hide in our cellar. No one goes there much.' The cellar was full of broken bikes and skates and scooters and stuff. They settled him behind the big box in the corner. Cressy went to fetch a blanket while Axel sneaked up to the kitchen. What should he make? He had to hurry before anyone came. He decided on lemon curd sandwiches and apple juice. As Axel slipped back towards the cellar door with the tray, a little inquisitive face appeared, peeping noiselessly through the banister rails – his troublesome cousin Truffle.

'So! Axel and Cressy are having a picnic without me,' thought Truffle. 'That's not fair!'

Cressy brought two pairs of pyjamas, one red and one blue; a fluffy toy cat; a needle and cotton; scissors; Savlon; a candle; matches; and some comics.

With all that and the feast Axel had made, the Unimouse was soon comfortable, though he was anxious about being discovered in the cellar. He said his name was Jorian. As dizzy as he was, he looked around at all the broken things in the cellar with great interest.

'What's all this? Why don't you fix these things?' he asked.

'No one knows how to,' said Cressy.

'And what is in this big box?'

The big old box in the corner belonged to Great Aunt Bryony. Inside were treasures from her sea voyage to Atlantis. No one had ever been able to open it. It had a digital combination lock.

Scuttling out into the wood, Truffle was cross, and looking for trouble. She was trying to find someone to tell about the secret picnic, and she wasn't being at all careful; she was just jumping around the fallen branches, grumbling.

'If I had lemon curd sandwiches, I'd share them,' she said to herself. This wasn't exactly true, but there was no one to point that out. 'I would invite everyone to the picnic. I would pass round the Hobnobs . . .'

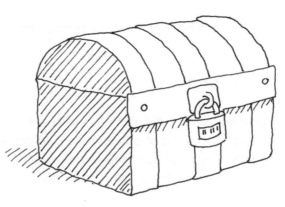

Flash! A big, hard, heavy, iron paw descended on her tail.

Her thoughts nearly stopped.

The sky spun and the big globes of rain from the tree tops dropped down like weights.

It was Bushey the Fox.

It was still only half past seven in the morning. At that moment, Sparky Wiremouse, doing a round of the tree houses after the storm with his bag of bulbs, fuses and fixings, knocked on the door of Oak Tree House. 'Thank you,' said Jorian. 'If my wings dry out, perhaps I can leave tonight.' Cressy and Axel left him to rest, and went to get some breakfast. And Truffle said to Bushey in a high, frightened whine,

'If you let me go I can show you where there are *two* nice juicy mice. . .'

Literacy activities using story opener *Jorian the Unimouse*

1. Group activity: speaking and listening

Ask the children to work in groups. Please ensure that children have learned how and why to take part in exploratory talk; your plenary sessions should require children to evaluate the quality of their discussion with one another. Problems within groups should be discussed in a whole class setting and suggestions taken for remedy. Use of the class ground rules for talk is essential and should be highlighted before group talk begins.

The first group activity is to talk and think together to decide on an *ending for the story*, without writing anything down at this stage. This can be a 'final' ending or a chapter ending. The children must call upon their imagination and creativity to devise ideas using some of the detail the story opener provides.

If you wish to provide some structure, ask the children to make decisions about:

*   What happens to Truffle?
*   How does Jorian the Unimouse stay hidden; or what happens if he is found?
*   What does Jorian do to repay the help Cressy and Axel have given him?

If needed to prompt thinking, provide groups with Talking Points (see p. 37).

2. Writing activities

Following group discussion, share responses to the story with the whole class. Show children the value of collaborating, which is not the same as copying. Ask the children to use drawing to capture their ideas based on their discussion. Writing activities can then be organised to address any area of literacy.

Talking Points: *Jorian the Unimouse*

In Jorian's backpack is a laptop, spanners, oil and a bike tyre repair kit.

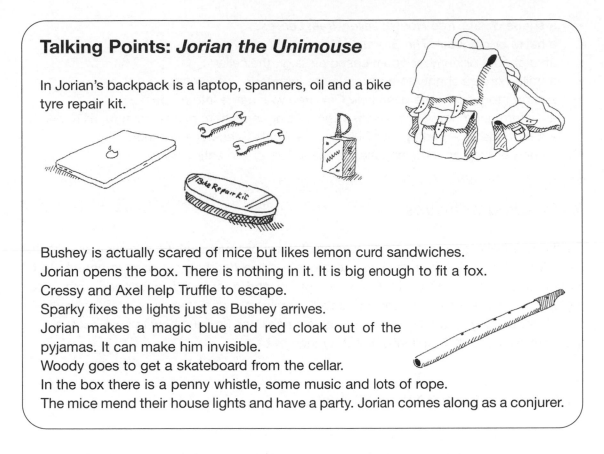

Bushey is actually scared of mice but likes lemon curd sandwiches.
Jorian opens the box. There is nothing in it. It is big enough to fit a fox.
Cressy and Axel help Truffle to escape.
Sparky fixes the lights just as Bushey arrives.
Jorian makes a magic blue and red cloak out of the pyjamas. It can make him invisible.
Woody goes to get a skateboard from the cellar.
In the box there is a penny whistle, some music and lots of rope.
The mice mend their house lights and have a party. Jorian comes along as a conjurer.

Suggestions for writing activities

- a story board using the group's ideas as a structure;
- group or individual story or chapter ending;
- an additional scene for the story;
- the story from Jorian's point of view;
- a play script of a scene from the story;
- a play script for puppets;
- a freeze-frame for the story as it is and also for their own ending;
- a description of each of the characters;
- a description of the setting for the story (an imaginary world);
- an annotated drawing of a cut-away vertical section of the tree house;
- a dialogue between Truffle and Cressy in which Truffle explains her behaviour;
- an instruction manual for opening the box in the cellar;
- a factual non-chronological report: tree houses, mice, foxes, oak trees, bikes;
- a fictional non-chronological report: *Unimice*; *About Oak Tree House*;
- an explanation of how to mend a bike puncture;
- the front page of *Mouse Times*, with a report of the storm and the damage caused;
- a timeline for the story, and an analysis of connectives used to move the story along;
- a list of the damage done by the storm and what will be needed to fix it;
- a postcard from one of the mice in the tree house describing the stormy night;
- an estate agent's description of the tree house, or the cellar;
- an advertisement for Sparky Wiremouse's electrical business;
- a recount – Cressy or Axel's diary, blog or email to a friend;
- a recount – Great Aunt Bryony's Sea Voyage to Atlantis;

- a shape poem: *Tree House*; *Fallen Tree*; *Leaves*;
- a haiku or cinquain: *The Storm*;
- an alphabet or number poem based on, e.g., the cellar;
- a ballad or sea shanty to accompany sailors on the sea voyage;
- a short story set in the past: how Oak Tree was made into a house;
- a performance poem or nonsense verse using repetition, rhyme, rhythm, alliteration;
- a set of riddles – perhaps for Bushey and Truffle to ask one another;
- a song or tune as a theme tune for characters or the entire story.

3. Reading activities

Children's initial discussion, and discussion of the subsequent writing activities, can be the basis for further reading. Individual and group reading can help children to contribute to further discussion in which texts are compared and contrasted, described, explained, preferences expressed with reasons, detail examined – whatever aspect of literacy your class is studying. A shared story is invaluable for children learning how to analyse, evaluate and communicate their opinions about a range of texts.

Suggestions for reading activities

- one another's written work;
- non-fiction texts for information, e.g. oak woods, tree houses, sea voyages;
- a range of fantasy stories;
- related poems in the form you wish to teach;
- play scripts;
- relevant web pages, e.g. information about storms and storm damage, oak trees.

For more information and an ending to the story of *Jorian the Unimouse*, see Further Reading.

Onyx Quest

In the fathomless cave below the summit of Crinkle Crags lived a dragon who took away cats.

The villagers of Rossett didn't seem to question it. Why did they put up with it? Were they all cowards, or didn't they care about their pets? Declan had once asked his father why they couldn't simply go and slay the dragon, or block up its cave.

'If we try to do that, or even keep all the cats safe indoors, it'll take away children instead.'

Hmm! Declan saw the force of this, but still didn't see why there couldn't be a fight.

'But we could all take swords, and if it was dead, we'd be safe?'

'Ah, – but – you see,' said his father, who obviously didn't really want to be talking about this, 'it isn't a dragon you can kill with swords. No. That wouldn't be the way of it.'

'OK, poison it then.'

'If only.' Declan's father, who was a slate miner, was waxing his big boots. He carried on steadily polishing around the holes where the laces went. 'It's been tried . . . I tell you son, the only person left who knows much about it is Millican Eaglesfield. There's not much chance of getting any sense out of him . . . better forget it, my lad. It's going on fine as it is.'

But it wasn't fine; people's cats kept getting taken. But Declan did forget it, for a while.

Millican Eaglesfield appeared in the village once a year or so, in heavy old clothes which seemed to be made of wool mixed with bracken and barley straw. Swapping the little, delicate carvings of creatures he had made during the long winter in the hills for cheese, dried fruit and flour, Millican accepted an old pair of shoes from the cobbler, and went on his way again.

And so the villagers never really spoke of the dragon. But at least they had organised what they thought was a good system to stop it striking at random. On the night of each new moon, a cat was chosen and marked with a special collar. Two days later, it was taken in a cat basket to the inaccessible rock ledge below the cave and left there. This system saved the worry that the dragon might blunder around the village and damage people and homes. It gave time for families to choose a new kitten. And it had the added advantage that no one ever saw the dragon, though some had heard it when the mountains were in the clouds, and fell walkers reported fleeting sightings on the darkest days of the year.

Everyone accepted this system for dealing with the dragon. Declan and Scout, who was his cousin, had been lucky. Their last cat had gone some years ago when they were too young to understand. The family had simply chosen another kitten and carried on. The replacement cat was the real problem, because she was just the right sort of cat. That is, irreplaceable. She was an alert, grey and fawn and cream, stripy but mottled, independent but friendly cat; and her name was Onyx.

And then it was the best time of the year; spring was moving up the valley, bringing leaves and insects and long fresh days. Declan's birthday approached. Declan and Scout were talking about it on their way home from school, taking it in turns to walk on the low walls of the houses each side of the street.

'Guess what I'm giving you this year? Nothing!' said Scout.

'Just what I wanted.'

This was the sort of conversation they liked. Scout had spent ages searching the internet and found a special kind of watch that told you not just the time, but where you were, and how high or low: almost like the opposite of a diver's watch; a mountain watch. And Declan knew that Scout wouldn't let his birthday go by without producing some kind of wonderful gadget.

Rossett village was not just near the mountains, it was in the mountains, and almost as high as you could go. No vehicles could traverse the steep slopes rising up to the summits of Bow Fell and Stonesty Pike, not even the quad bikes the farmers used to manage the hardy Herdwick sheep that managed to thrive on the cold slopes. The Herdwicks which Scout's family farmed had the ability, unusual in sheep, to find their own way home. The only way that you could get higher than the village was on your own two feet, walking, scrambling or climbing. Declan and Scout were adept mountain walkers and both belonged to the Mountain Rescue, helping to round up the tourists who were forever straying too high or wandering off into the mist. But today, the tops were clear, and above the fathomless cave Crinkle Crags looked sharp, dark and inviting.

'Shall we go for a climb . . .?'

'Jam sandwich first.'

'OK – race you to your house.'

So they were laughing, Scout and Declan, as they shoved each other through the door. On the chair by the window was Onyx. She was sitting up quite straight, with not a whisker moving. She was wearing a strange, distinctive, vermilion collar.

It was Onyx's turn. In just two days, she would go to the dragon's ledge.

Literacy activities using story opener *Onyx Quest*

1. Group activity: speaking and listening

Ask the children to work in groups. Ensure that children have learned how and why to take part in exploratory talk. Closing plenary sessions require children to evaluate the quality and range of their discussion with one another. Problems within groups should be discussed and suggestions for progress aired. Use of the class ground rules for talk is essential and the rules should be highlighted before group talk begins.

The first group activity is to talk and think together to decide on an *ending for the story*, without writing anything down at this stage. Ask the children to devise a plan in which Declan and Scout try to save Onyx. This can be a 'final' ending or a chapter ending. The children must call upon their imagination and creativity to devise ideas using some of the detail the story opener provides.

Allow plenty time for discussion before providing *Onyx Quest Planning*, p. 43 (if you are going to use this). Once groups are given this resource, the nature of their discussion will change.

Make it clear that the rescue plan cannot involve resorting to violence, but requires some sort of thoughtful or clever resolution in which the dragon is tricked or distracted by cunning,

> ### Talking Points: *Onyx Quest*
>
> Declan and Scout try to persuade their parents to help Onyx.
> The rescue has to be kept secret.
> Millican Eaglesfield turns up and offers some help.
> It is spring; the weather will make a difference.
> Friends might help.
> Declan might get some useful birthday presents.
> Onyx can make a difference.
> We know why the dragon wants the cats.
> We can say what the dragon looks like and what powers it has.
> The dragon has some serious weaknesses.
> There is only one dragon and only one cave.
> The dragon must be defeated but cannot be killed.

or by the children winning a battle of wits. Note that 'Scout' can be male or female, and the children's ages are not specified. Sometimes children prefer to put themselves in the story; in this case they can change a character's name to 'I'.

If you wish, ask children to think together to discuss some of the Talking Points provided. These are suggestions – your own may be more relevant to the children in your class.

After discussion, or if needed to prompt thinking, provide *each child* with the resource *Onyx Quest Planning*. Using this, groups choose three items to help with their quest. The children can decide if they wish to give any one item magical properties. Some groups may want to incorporate more sophisticated equipment e.g. an iPod or mobile phone; this is fine as long as the items are used to some effect in the story. That is, 'The dragon put on its iPod headphones and flew away to be happy ever after'; 'They called up the Army on the mobile' really will not do!

2. *Writing activities*

Ask children to draw pictures using ideas based on their discussion, then share with class-mates. Writing activities can be organised to address areas of literacy suitable to your class.

Suggestions for writing activities

- a story board using the group's ideas as a structure;
- group or individual story or chapter ending;
- an additional scene for the story;
- the story from Scout's point of view;
- a play script of a scene from the story;
- a play script for puppets, or an oral story narrative;
- a freeze-frame for the story as it is and also for their own ending;
- a detailed description of each of the characters;
- a description of the setting for the story (an imaginary world);
- an annotated drawing of the village, farms, crags and the cave system;
- a dialogue in which Declan tries to persuade his father to help save Onyx;
- an instruction manual for a mountain watch;
- a factual non-chronological report: cats, Herdwick sheep, Mountain Rescue services;
- a fictional non-chronological report: dragons, Rossett village;
- an explanation of how to look after a cat, or a donkey, or a sheep dog;
- news page with farming news, quarrying article, item about cats previously taken;
- a timeline for the story, and an analysis of connectives used to move the story along;
- a list of what will be needed to set off on the Quest;
- a text, email, card or letter from Declan to a friend describing what they are about to do;
- an estate agent's description of the cave, Scout's farm or Declan's house in the village;
- a recount – Declan, Onyx or the dragon's diary or blog;
- a recount – Millican Dalton's previous meeting with the dragon;
- a shape poem: *Dragon*; *Mountain*; *Herdwick*; *Scout*;
- a haiku or cinquain; mountain storm;
- a short story set in the past: how the Dragon first stole a cat;
- a performance poem or nonsense verse using repetition, rhyme, rhythm, alliteration;

Onyx Quest planning

Our group's names are:

1. Special equipment: choose three items.

One of them has magical properties. Which object? What can it do?

Compass	Gold key	Donkey	Sheep dog	Flute
Illustrated story book	Cloaks	Mountain watches	Tent	Torch
Herdwick wool blanket	Map of the cave	Binoculars	Dice	Mountain walking stick

2. The main characters

(name/age/good at/likes/disklikes)

3. About the dragon

(appearance/likes/dislikes/strengths/weaknesses/magical powers)

4. What happens at Declan's house?

What do the children do in the two days before Onyx has to leave?

- a set of riddles – perhaps for child characters to ask the dragon;
- a PowerPoint presentation: *Onyx Quest*;
- a song or tune as a theme tune for characters or the entire story.

3. Reading activities

Children's initial discussion, and discussion of the subsequent writing activities, can be the basis for further reading. Ask children to analyse, evaluate and share reasoned opinions about one another's work.

Suggestions for reading

- one another's written work;
- non-fiction texts for information e.g. *Herdwick Sheep*; *Caves and Caving*; *Mountain Walking*; *Map Reading*; *The Lake District*;
- fiction texts for information, e.g. *Mythology Concerning Dragons*;
- a range of fantasy stories;
- related poems in the form you wish to teach;
- play scripts;
- relevant web pages e.g. information about life in the Lake District Fells, Scottish Highlands or Welsh Mountains.

Conclusions

Children need us to help them learn to use talk as much as they need help with reading and writing. Talk and thinking with others offers resources the child draws upon to achieve reading and writing fluency. Reading and writing are not just more effective but actually more possible if they are based on group discussion. The use of stories and other texts, coupled with motivating talk-based activities, can help children to move readily into seeing the point of, and making use of, more abstract knowledge about language.

Speaking and listening, reading and writing, should come first. Stories, poems, web pages, a wide range of written texts and spoken ideas should be both the stimulus for and the outcomes of literacy. The rigmarole about 'employ polysyllabic adjectives'; 'find and use new and interesting words and phrases, including story language'; 'summarise and shape material and ideas from different sources to write convincing and informative non-narrative texts'; 'choose and combine words, images and other features for particular effects' – is sterile; and yet it's what children are asked to study, every day. These things are arcane analytical devices for the scholar, not ways into loving reading and writing for the child. Teachers don't want to start by dissecting stories and texts, but by helping children to create them. Through a speaking and listening approach children can naturally achieve literacy without being burdened with ridiculous Learning Intentions.

I think that children can either become literate in primary school, or can be taught the nuts and bolts of 'Literacy'. For some, reading and writing comes easily. For most, it doesn't, and for all children, Learning Intentions should be primarily to do with reading things they want to read, discussing ideas and having a chance to do their own writing about things they want to write about. What teachers can do is help children to want to, and be able to, read and write a widening range of texts.

Why, instead, are we teaching children aged 7–11 years such horrendous things as 'Show relationships of time, reason and cause, through subordination and connectives'? 'Write complex sentences, which capture cause and effect in explanations and alternative viewpoints in argument and persuasion'? Simply because the learning of such things can be quantified and tested, and schools can be ranked on what they have made children achieve. We can measure things, but doing so stops learning in the same way that finding out how butterflies work stops them flying. Focused talk about reading and writing, however, generates and sustains interest. Encouraging children to articulate their thinking, and to listen and respond to others, creates a buzzy 'workshop' atmosphere in which literacy thrives.

Chapter 5

TALK FOR LEARNING ACROSS THE CURRICULUM

This chapter describes tried-and-tested strategies which can be used to incorporate the powerful tools of speaking and listening into any curriculum area. Strategies described here are: Talking Points, Notes and Queries, Annotated Drawing and Question Trail.

Speaking and listening strategies for curriculum learning

1. Talking Points

A strategy which I and other teachers have found works well for almost any curriculum topic is the use of Talking Points. Talking Points are statements which children can agree or disagree with; or the group can decide it is 'unsure'. Shared uncertainty is a valuable stimulus for thinking. Group discussion ensures that a range of points of view are heard and considered; Talking Points support exploratory talk. They can be used to bring out ideas at the beginning or at the end of a lesson or topic. There can be just one or two Talking Points, or many more if you want children to really focus on a topic in depth.

Talking Points discussions can expand to fill more than the time available – it is usually best to look for signs that some groups have come to the end of their discussion, and finish there, so that motivation and curiosity are maintained. Similarly, group feedback can be lengthy. A useful strategy is to ask a group to explain their thinking on one point, then ask them to choose another group to follow on. You don't need a summary or explanation until a range of opinions has been heard.

Until children learn how to discuss ideas, they tend to move very readily to agreement. Talking Points resources can end with a drawing activity which provides more for the group to think about while others are still talking. After discussion, ask a group for examples of points which they felt *unsure* about or which they thought were interesting.

You can devise your own Talking Points for topics; you can ask children to suggest talking points to share with other groups. Some science examples are provided here.

(See also Further Reading).

Talking Points: Light

Think together to decide whether these are true or false; or if you are unsure. Ask everyone for opinions, and give your reasons.

1 Light is a form of energy.

2 Light can travel through water, air and space.

3 The sun is the only light source on our planet.

4 Things that give out light (light sources) are always hot.

5 The moon is a giant reflector of light.

6 Light makes things easier to see, but we can still see when it's dark.

7 Dark is a form of energy which is weaker than light.

8 Rainbows show us what is mixed to make ordinary white light.

9 Surfaces absorb (soak up) light and reflect only some of it. A red door absorbs most colours and reflects only red.

10 You really are upside-down in a spoon.

11 Opaque things make sharp shadows by absorbing light.

12 Your shadow is sewn onto your feet.

13 You can get coloured shadows.

Think together to draw a picture of how our eyes work.
Label everything you draw and write a note to explain what it does.

Think together to write down as many words as you can which describe light.

Talking Points: Materials

Think together to decide whether these are true or false, or if you are unsure. Ask everyone for opinions and give your reasons.

1   All materials come from the resources of the earth.

2   Some materials we use are natural or unprocessed.

3   Some materials are manufactured or processed. This takes energy.

4   Soil, water, air and light are materials.

5   Bricks, fabrics and metals are all processed materials.

6   Plastic, like money, grows on trees.

7   Glass is made from sand.

8   Paper is a mat of wood fibres. It is easy to recycle.

9   We can each name a material we like, say what natural material it is made of, and describe its properties.

10   Most metals have magnetic properties.

11   Synthetic fabrics like foam or polyester can be dangerous.

12   We can think of three different materials that might be used to make lampshades, bottles, or shopping bags.

13   You cannot throw things away because there is no such place as 'away'.

14   Some materials cost more than others.

15   Our bodies are made from the same materials as a plant's.

Think together to draw a whole range of drinks containers, saying what materials they could be made of, and the advantages and disadvantages of each.

Talking Points: Plant life

Think together to decide whether these are true or false; or if you are unsure. Ask everyone for opinions, and give your reasons.

1   Animals could not survive without plants.

2   Plants need water, light and air to survive.

3   Leaves contain green chemicals which can collect energy from light.

4   Plants mainly get water from rain on their leaves.

5   The plant grows by getting food from the soil.

6   Plants have flowers so that they can make copies of themselves.

7   All plants have flowers.

8   Flowers use scent and colour to attract insects.

9   Pollen is another name for seed.

10   Plants need insects to take away and bring pollen.

11   The holder for seeds on a plant is called a fruit.

12   It's best for seeds to grow close by their parent plant.

13   Plants make lots of seeds so that there is food for animals.

14   Seeds need water and air to germinate.

15   Seeds need light to germinate.

16   Some seeds need fire or frost to help them germinate.

Think together to draw a plant, labelling all the parts you know, and saying what is the job of each part in the plant.

Talking Points: Ourselves as animals

Think together to decide whether these are true or false, or if you are unsure. Ask everyone for opinions and give your reasons.

1   Humans are the smartest animals on the planet.

2   People need water, air and food to survive.

3   Our bodies are made from the same materials as a plant's.

4   There are lots of things we can do to stay healthy.

5   Our teeth are always covered in bacteria.

6   Exercise is for competitive people and is nothing to do with health.

7   You are wasting time when you are asleep.

8   Our skin is waterproof and helps to keep us at the same temperature.

9   Calcium for our bones is found in milk, cheese, oranges and salmon.

10   We have lots of blood which sloshes around inside us.

11   We breathe in only oxygen, and breathe out only carbon dioxide.

12   We belong to a group of animals called mammals.

Think together to decide on two fives:

•   five differences between plants and animals;

•   five senses that we use to help us make sense of the world around us.

Can you think of an interesting way you can present your ideas to the class?

2. Notes and Queries

Notes and Queries are the children's starting ideas (Notes) and the things they want to know (Queries). Bringing out such ideas as you start a topic helps each child to understand that their own knowledge is of value. This strategy enables every child to share ideas, not just the ones who are chosen in a hands-up session. And children need to hear and experience things many times in order to make sense of them; listening to the ideas of their classmates is a very good start.

Start by choosing an appropriate resource which will interest the children and motivate them; something that they can look at, touch, hear, smell or do; or a large clear image.

Show the children your resource. Encourage children to look at the resource and talk informally before you begin.

Now ask the children to use exploratory talk with their group; think together to write down or share:

- Notes: three things that they *already know* about the resource or topic
- Queries: three *questions* to which they would like answers.

Example

A Year 4 group were asked to observe an image of the Egyptian goddess Bastet.

Notes

It's a Siamese cat. The cat is wearing earrings and a necklace. It is not very furry.

Queries

How did they pierce its ears? Why is it sitting still? Who is its owner?

Whole-class work can be based on this bank of ideas and questions. Ask each group in turn to share (read aloud) their 'Notes'. Provide post-its and ask children, working and talking with a partner, to go around the tables reading the questions others have written. If they can answer the question, do so and leave their answer note, signed, on the table.

Ask groups to look at their questions and the suggested answers. Ask each group to read a question and answer – or answers. With the whole class, discuss answers. Look for reasons, evidence and experience. Ask children who provided answers to explain their thinking. In this way children can begin to see that others in their class really can contribute to their understanding.

After this starter activity you can link children's questions to your presentation of new information.

Further activities based on Notes and Queries discussion

Ask children to:

- **Categorise** their questions:

  - *Which questions about Bastet can we investigate?*
    How old is the cat? What is its name? What colour is it? Why is it wearing jewellery? Why are its ears so big?

  - *Which questions have imaginative answers that are a matter of opinion?*
    Is it a friendly cat? Does it catch mice? What is it listening to? What does it like to eat?

- Choose a question to investigate or research using books, the internet, asking other classes or at home.
- Feedback information about the quality of the group talk; ask children for examples of good listening, sharing information, devising questions. Who learned from a classmate?
- Create a display with the questions as riddles on cards, answers underneath; or use questions to compile a quiz; make a mini-book about the resource; or a book for younger children; or a 'did you know' leaflet for parent's evening.

3. Annotated Diagrams

Drawing a picture is always a good way to get thinking started, especially if children talk and work within a group. Most curriculum areas lend themselves to drawing. The value of annotated diagrams lie in enabling the child to represent their ideas graphically, adding the words that indicate their understanding. Drawing enables children to examine the limits of their knowledge and understanding.

Children can be asked to draw annotated diagrams as a new topic starts, and then again after the unit of work. They can compare these diagrams and identify where progress has been made. The diagrams can be paper based or electronic. They can be simple or really complicated; they can take a few minutes or be built up over several sessions. Children can use colour simply for emphasis, or in a more sophisticated way to provide a key or to relate aspects of the diagram.

Teaching annotated drawing involves teaching a progression of skills and understanding:

1   what an annotated diagram is;
2   how to annotate pre-drawn diagrams from books or electronic material;
3   how to draw simple diagrams that help to convey their ideas;
4   where and when to add colour which gives meaning;
5   how to draw diagrams and add *given* vocabulary or labels;
6   how to draw diagrams and add *own* vocabulary or labels;
7   how to draw and annotate more complex diagrams starting with a blank sheet – with their group;
8   to compile more complex annotated diagrams starting with a blank sheet – individually.

Children need direct instruction in these things. Start by providing a selection of fiction and non-fiction texts and IWB resources which use annotated diagrams. Ask groups to think together to point out key features – clear drawing, labels, use of colour, ideas or descriptions, concise but in-depth information. Work through the list above one step at a time giving direct input on the skills needed. The crucial thing is that ultimately *children do the drawing* and *create the annotations*.

What annotated diagrams can we draw in Science?

Science 1

Draw and annotate equipment used for collecting data, e.g. data logger, thermometer, clinometer, sweep net, soil sieves; or investigation equipment, e.g. for separating mixtures to explain what each part does.

Draw and annotate a graph, table or chart using data collected, and annotate to show how the data is conveyed, to show understanding of units, the axes, the information in the body of the table, etc.

Science 2

How do we . . . breathe, digest food, think, hear, see, smell scents, feel with our fingers, run, keep our teeth healthy?
Draw and annotate the heart/what is inside our bones/a plant and how it works.
Draw and annotate what lives in an oak tree/a meadow/a forest/a pond.
Show how insects pollinate flowers/different ways that seeds are dispersed.
The secret life of bacteria or yeast cells.

Science 3

Soil from the top down.
Solids, liquids and gases – changes between states using particle theory.
What happens when sugar dissolves in water.
The difference between a mixture and a new material made by irreversible change.

Science 4

What's inside a battery/bulb/wire/motor/LED.
Gravity and its effect on ourselves, the earth and the moon.
Pushes/pulls/friction and surfaces.
Light and shadows/colours in white light.
How strings, pipes and drums make sound.
How the earth moves in space.

Annotated diagrams can help children to discuss current and developing ideas, and can help both you and the child decide what they need to learn next. Activities involving annotating *text* also benefit from group discussion.

4. Question Trail

This strategy is based on the game 'Consequences'. Each group begins with a blank piece of paper, writing their group name at the top, and folding the paper over to cover it.

(Perceived anonymity can lead to inappropriate responses! Ensure children are aware that the papers will be used by other children in the class.)

On display provide some *question openers*:

What if . . .? Why do . . .? Why don't . . .? How can . . .? Where . . .? Does anyone know . . .? Can you tell . . .? What can we . . .? Do you think that . . .? Can you imagine if . . .? Which . . .? What reason . . .? What would be the outcome if . . .? Are these . . .?

Ask children to read question openers out and think about uses. Provide a resource that will start your topic; something to look at, touch or hear; perhaps a poem, story extract or short piece of text; a picture, diagram or video clip. Help the children to think about the lesson focus.

Ask the groups to use exploratory talk to think of a *good question* – that is, something thought provoking. Write their question at the top of the paper and fold it over. When all groups are ready, pass the paper on to another group. The receiving group reads the question, discusses their answer and writes it down. They then discuss and record a further question, fold over and hold up the paper, ready to pass it on. At this point, group members may need to cross the classroom to swap papers because all groups are working to their own time, some taking longer than others over discussion. Carry on with the discussion and recording of answers and questions for five minutes; or until you can tell that it has gone on long enough. During this time, check papers for inappropriate answers; remove 'offending' items and substitute a fresh paper. Also, try to choose a Question Trail which you can use in the closing plenary. Finally, stop the class and ask all children to return to their places. Ask groups to pass the papers to their original owners.

Each group will have a list of questions and answers – a Question Trail. Ask your chosen group to read theirs out. Discuss any ideas that arise with the whole class. Comment on the quality and range of the questions. If time, all Question Trails can be read out.

Further activities based on Question Trail discussion

- Ask children to type a Question Trail, editing and improving it.
- Research answers to factual questions.
- Type questions only; use them to interview other children or parents.
- Create a group story board or poem using imaginative questions.
- Transfer questions and answers to PowerPoint slides. Illustrate slides and collect them into a class resource. Write a story based on the slides.

Example: Question Trail based on Frank Stella's picture *Hyena Stomp*

(see Further Reading)

Is it a pyramid or a tunnel?
A tunnel. What would happen if you flew into it?
You would be in colour world. What shapes can you see?
Triangle/square/trapezium/spiral. What is at the end of the tunnel?
What do you think? How far away is it?

Conclusions

A range of strategies can help children to share their ideas. There are many more – talk partners, concept cartoons, puppets, mind maps and concept maps for example (see Further Reading) and you can generate your own. Board games (Taboo, Who Wants to Be a Millionaire, Trivial Pursuit) can be adapted to provide a stimulus for discussion. There are online games, mobile phone or computer games, visualisers, books and websites, all of which can support educationally effective talk.

Talk strategies are often described as 'assessment tools' because they offer the chance to evaluate an individual child's understanding. If we can forget collecting data for a while, we can think of the children's discussion as a process, an opportunity for talking meaningfully with their classmates, and a chance to experience the mix of hesitancy and firmly-held opinion that is a characteristic of exploratory talk. Enabling a child to give and hear reasons and to negotiate ideas is not just so that we can check knowledge against a particular target or level; but so that the child actually learns to reason – and learns the value of reasoning with others.

Simple strategies such as those described here can be rapidly integrated into the usual work of your classroom. Such sessions should be integral and should enhance learning, as with ICT use. It takes some determined planning to do this; you have to be on 'a mission'. Talk always takes longer than you'd expect, so you really have to allocate time for it. And you have to know that the children's talk will be of value. So, when you have a speaking and listening activity which really supports your topic and you put 'exploratory talk' on your lesson plan, it isn't just a blank space – it's probably the best bit.

Chapter 6

TALK ABOUT OPINIONS AND FEELINGS

As well as discussing factual information, children need to learn to talk about their opinions, attitudes, beliefs and feelings. They may hold tenuous or surprisingly strong opinions. They may have reflected on ideas or may simply be repeating what they have heard. Attitudes and beliefs represent their cultural history, which includes their school experience. Behaviour is a reflection of these things. If children are to discuss their behaviour and that of others, they need a robust talk structure which enables all points of view to be heard. A working knowledge of exploratory talk can support children as they account for themselves or listen to others in order to try to understand things.

During their primary years children will meet both positive experiences and problems. Through these they must learn about friendships, bullying, telling the truth, family celebrations or problems, difficulty with school work, loss, grief, happiness, taking responsibility and generally growing up. That is, they must become socialised. Having the chance to discuss opinions and perspectives with classmates can help children to hear and consider a range ideas. They can begin to see that their own experiences can usefully be shared and may be part of a more general social context. Choices may become clearer if they can think things through with others.

A story setting for problems helps to keep things impersonal whilst offering the chance to rehearse and share complex feelings and ideas. In this chapter a story is used as the basis for group discussion on the theme of *friendship.*

Some Friends: a story for discussion

Stories can help children take part in discussion in the curriculum areas of *communication* and *social understanding*. Before reading the story *Some Friends* with your class, please ensure that children are in their groups and ready to take part in discussion. Rehearse the class rules for exploratory talk. Decide in advance which discussion activity (or activities) you would like groups to undertake. In this example, children have the chance to consider and share their individual ideas before taking part in whole class discussion. Provide a copy of the story for each group, and then read it aloud.

Some Friends

Orla thought she was lucky. She had a funny baby brother who was just starting to crawl, and her family had just got a dog. They had been along to the Dog Rescue Centre and chosen a wonderful, long legged black and white puppy. Orla called him Fizzy. Fizzy was a bit nervous, but lots of fun. On Sunday, Orla was allowed to go to the park to take Fizzy for a walk. 'Keep him on the lead,' said her Dad. 'You know what he's like!'

Orla was running round a big tree in the park when her friends Janis and Roxanne came by. 'Oh, isn't he lovely!' 'Why is he on a lead – does he bite?' 'Course not.' said Orla. 'Where are you going?' 'To watch a film,' said Janis. 'My cousin's coming round too. Here – look at this.' Orla looked at the DVD case. She didn't notice Roxanne lean down and unclip Fizzy's lead. She looked up in horror to see the puppy dashing off towards the climbing frame. 'He's not allowed off the lead!'

'Oh let him play, it's good exercise,' said Roxanne. Orla dashed after the dog, fear making her run faster. Just then there was a tremendous clatter and a loud whoosh as a helicopter flew overhead. Startled, Fizzy charged off towards the wood at the edge of the park. Orla stopped dead. At the top of the wood was the main road. 'Help me catch him!' she shouted to her friends. Neither of them moved. 'Come on, boy!' called Roxanne carelessly. 'Oh, just leave him. He'll come back when he's ready.' 'Sorry – got to go – my cousin's waiting . . .' Janis waved. 'And hey! I'm not supposed to get my trainers muddy . . .' Chattering, they left without even looking back. Orla was alone in the park.

She called Fizzy, trying to sound calm instead of scared. She ran along the edge of the wood. He had vanished. But! Here was help – coming along the path were Mitek and Iain, kicking a football to each other. Orla rushed up to them. 'My dog . . . run away . . . only a puppy . . . doesn't know where he is . . . please help . . .'. They both looked into the wood for a moment, kicking the ball against the trees. 'I don't like dogs,' said Mitek. Iain laughed. 'But he might get run over! Or cause a car crash,' said Orla desperately. They made loud car crash noises, bashing into each other. Orla couldn't believe it. 'You're not going to help, are you? Please, shhh! You'll probably frighten him even more.' 'Oh well, if we're not wanted,' said Iain. 'We can't stay anyway. We have to practice.' And with a final boot of the ball at the nearest tree, they left.

Orla suddenly felt cold and weak. She sat down on the grass and hid her face in her hands. What would her parents say? What if Fizzy got hurt – or killed? It would be her fault. She was shaky and scared and she even thought she might be sick.

'Oy,' said a voice. She looked up. It was Tom. He was wearing his usual grubby t-shirt and his hair was tangled and getting in his eyes. Everyone was a bit scared of Tom in school. No one would sit next to him because he was so badly behaved, and his clothes smelled funny. For some reason he was carrying an empty tin of baby milk, the sort her brother drank. Maybe he wanted to steal her pocket money. But at this moment she didn't care what happened to her.

'What's up?' he said.

'My puppy – he ran away in the wood – he won't come back . . .'

Tom narrowed his eyes and scanned the steep bank of trees; they could both hear cars whooshing by on the main road. He shrugged. Orla hid her face in her hands, and when she looked up again, he'd vanished.

Why would anyone expect a disaster like Tom to help? thought Orla. She got up and tiptoed along the edge of the trees, calling 'Fizzy!' very gently – and quite hopelessly. Along the whole length of the park she went, then back again for what seemed hours, stopping and listening, and by now, sure she would never see Fizzy again. She would just keep looking till dark, or even after dark, and never go home again. Eventually she began to cry; and then stopped, because even that was pointless with no one to care. People came and went in the park. The sky began to go pale and it was getting very cold. It was no good. She sat down and rubbed her eyes hard. Hopeless.

'Oy.'

She looked up – and there was Tom again, sticks in his hair and his face grimy – and, next to him, in the same dishevelled condition – Fizzy – with Tom's grubby fingers firmly through his collar; '– this your dog?' Tom asked.

'Yes! Yes!' She leapt up. She clipped on the lead.

'Oh, wow! How did you do that! Oh – Fizzy. Thank you, Tom!' How could things go from bad to good in an instant like that? She jumped up and down and round in a circle, laughing. She thought about running home and not telling about the awful afternoon, so that her parents still trusted her with Fizzy. But now – Tom was walking away. She ran after him. 'Where are you going now? Can't you stay?'

'Going to the shop – sister needs this stuff.'

'Oh, right.' That explained the tin. 'But Tom! It's Sunday. They shut at four.'

He stared at her, and she suddenly recognised the same dreadful feeling that she had only just got over herself. No milk for his baby sister – almost worse than losing a puppy. She hesitated, but only for a fraction of a second. Then she laughed aloud and pulled Tom's arm. 'Come on! My house. My kid brother has that sort of milk. We've got a new tin you can have!'

Instantly, Tom grinned; something about things made Fizzy begin to bark furiously; and then all three of them started running. They just flew.

And Tom insisted on paying for the baby milk, even though Orla's Dad wanted him to take it for free, in return for his help.

On Monday morning, Miss Kay asked the class to write about 'Friendship'. Sitting next to Janis, Orla thought about it. What was it that made someone your friend? How could you tell who was a friend? Would they always be your friend? What made friends unkind to one another sometimes, and what turned strangers into friends? Was it a good idea to forgive friends who weren't always perfect? Was she herself a good friend to people? If so, would that make them act like a good friend to her? Wondering why she felt a bit worried about choosing him, but feeling defiant about it, and very sure, Orla started to draw a picture of Tom.

Discussion activities based on *Some Friends*

1. Orla's questions

Ask the groups to discuss their ideas about the questions at the end of the story.

2. Talking Points – what do you think? Why?

1   Orla should not be allowed out on her own with the puppy.
2   She will not be friends with Tom for long.
3   The boys in the story are all unpleasant.
4   Janis is vain.
5   Orla hesitates before offering Tom the baby milk because she really wants to pretend nothing went wrong when she gets home.
6   Orla will never trust her friends again.
7   Someone who has only helped you once is not a friend.
8   We can think of examples of when we have helped others, or others have helped us.

3. Notes and Queries

Talk together to write down three ideas and three questions about:

a)   the characters in the story

and/or

b)   friendship.

4. Annotated Drawing

1. Using the illustrations provided, draw speech bubbles, and separate thought bubbles. Show differences between what characters are thinking and saying.

2. Each choose a scene from the story to draw. Decide together how to annotate your pictures with information from the story. Add speech and thought bubbles.

3. Draw an annotated diagram in which you create a new scene for the story. Who else could come along, after the boys, but before Tom? Why don't they help? Perhaps it's another dog walker?

5. Question Trail

Ask groups to choose one of Orla's questions from the end of the story. Write it down and swap papers. Ask groups to discuss responses; then decide on and write their own answer to the question. Think up a further question using points from the discussion, only using Orla's questions if stuck. Question openers: 'what do you think –?', 'what if –?', 'can you say more about –?' might be useful.

Share the Question Trails with the whole class and discuss ideas.

6. Name Swap

Ask groups to discuss the idea of swapping all the girl's names in the story for boy's names, and vice versa. Try reading it out together. Does it work? If not, why not? Discuss ideas about stereotyping, roles and expectations.

An example of talk about feelings

Transcript 9: Teasing is an extract from discussion between a teacher and two Year 6 children whose behaviour had disrupted others.

Transcript 9: Teasing

T:	Right, you two effectively stopped eight people doing the end of that lesson properly, messing about. Have you got a reason for it?
Shane:	Nothing. Except for Gina was teasing.
T:	What was she saying to you?
Shane:	Um, that – um, calling me rabbit. I don't mind being called a rabbit, but they go too far with it, they go, oh we'll go and shoot him. And, go back to the place you came from, go back to the wild.
Nicky:	Or transform.
Shane:	Yes – don't transform back into a human, stay as you are. Rabbit. That's too far.

T: It's hard to deal with that isn't it? Because if you say nothing, what happens
          if you ignore them, could you try that?
Shane: *(doubtfully)* – yes . . . it's Gina says it, everyone joins in.
T: Why do you think that is – I don't understand it?
Shane: Because I've got big front teeth.
T: You've got lovely teeth; you're just an ordinary human being.
Shane: There's many people in the class that have got bigger teeth than me and
          they don't call them anything.

Comment

These children were familiar with exploratory talk, which is used here with the teacher who asks some genuine questions. She also asks for reasons and information. The children were able to explain what had happened in a way that helped the teacher to understand some classroom undercurrents, and usefully helped Shane to share his feelings. It is inevitable that friendships will be tested and teasing will happen; but providing children with discussion skills enables them to make better sense of their own position and that of others, and may help to pre-empt some problems. Stories and subsequent discussion of opinions and feelings can help children trust one another and their teacher in ways that ultimately make learning more possible.

Conclusions

Individual or group writing, reading, art work or discussion of social issues can draw on the shared thinking of discussion groups. *Some Friends* is a modified *Good Samaritan* story. Difficult issues can be discussed by using such stories, in which the characters find themselves in a range of problematic situations. Children can relate to story characters and use discussion to develop understanding. It is helpful for children to hear a range of points of view. They also need to realise that there may not be agreement when the class is discussing ideas and opinions rather than factual information. Despite this, it is still crucial to talk through issues so that children learn to account for themselves honestly, and to respect other perspectives.

Chapter 7

DECISION LEARNING

There is an implicit conflict between the teacher's responsibility for control and their responsibility for learning: one treats pupils as receivers and the other treats them as makers.

(Barnes, 1992: 176)

Creative teachers, creative learners

As Douglas Barnes says, we have the responsibility to control children – there is no way round it. Teachers who are themselves creative, or 'makers', as he puts it, can let children be makers too. Not just sometimes, but often. What I call 'decision learning' is a strategy in which teachers create, plan and organise an environment so that children decide what they will do with their time. They work together to ask and answer questions and to pursue ideas of interest. We can offer such choice. We can set up conditions in which children make their own understanding as they raise questions, discuss what to do and what they are doing, and enlist group involvement in decision making and problem solving.

We might know, for example, that 'like' poles of magnets repel one another; but for a child, that is *new* knowledge, which must be created in individual minds. Children must also create the original combinations of recently introduced and existing vocabulary that will explain their new thinking; they also need the chance to ask further questions.

Creativity in this sense means learning. It is a product of imaginative and original teaching. Teaching in this sense includes thorough planning to establish a focused and sustainable learning environment in which the powerful tools of spoken language are harnessed to the learner's advantage. In such a setting, there is an increased chance that a teacher can engage children in one-to-one instruction, explanation and discussion of ideas.

Imagine your class coming into school, each one of them knowing just what they want to and are going to do, and setting about learning with no introduction or prompting. At least once in a while, we can organise this; giving children the chance to decide what they will do, to move between activities, talk about and share their ideas, take their time, and generally learn in an organic way that sticks in the mind. By cutting through the timetable whilst retaining curriculum learning objectives, we can foster independent and collaborative work, provide real motivation and also create opportunities to have the sort of close, friendly conversations which both teachers and children love. We can provide individualised chances to get to grips with some important parts of the primary curriculum.

The importance of this sort of work is that it provides exceptional opportunities for the individual child to talk to others in a range of contexts, to listen and think aloud and alone, to work steadily with other children and to reflect on learning. It is inclusive of all abilities and aptitudes. It can provide you with invaluable opportunities to hear what children think, so that subsequent planning can be based on an understanding of every child's needs. Learning can take place through talk, with a high level of motivation fuelling the child's engagement.

Children who are used to highly structured school days may need to adjust to making their own decisions about learning. This chapter provides a plan for building up children's awareness of what is expected of them and 'what they can expect' when asked to take decisions about their own learning.

Aims of decision learning

One aim is to create a busy, engaged classroom community where tasks are achievable and interesting, and lead to further questions, enquiries and discussions. In addition there is the expectation that all members of the class will be supported by all others, in the understanding that learning will happen for everyone, not just for some. By working together, everyone can do better than if each child worked alone; the class can take pride in itself as a unit, and each child can feel that they have made a significant contribution to class achievement.

Activities and resources for decision learning

For each group, there should be a choice of at least two activities. So for ten groups of three children you might provide:

- 15 shoe boxes, plastic baskets or bowls containing resources for a complete activity including instructions or prompts for thinking, such as Talking Points. Plan to resource three activities; put together five baskets of resources for each activity.
- Computers with appropriate sites or software, digital cameras, video recorder, sound recorder, visualise, whiteboard resources.
- Craft resources for creating mini-books, a class big book or carpet book, posters, observational drawings, rubbings, collages.
- Appropriate books, magazines and space to read.
- Relevant jigsaws, board games and card games.
- Cross-curricular activities to help make links.

Organising an afternoon of decision learning (2 hours)

Previous week: Plan and collect resources; discuss ground rules for collaborative work; introduce the topic and suggest children might bring relevant resources from home.

Previous session – ½ hour: Discuss ground rules with reasons; provide a list of possible activities; establish groups.

Ask children to talk with their group to plan which activity to do first and why and agree this with you to check resources are not stretched. Initially it is important to provide a *minimum* time limit of 15–20 minutes for activities. This may seem a big constraint, but children have to learn to really engage with what they are doing, and they will not do this by starting to do four or five things in a half-hearted way.

An afternoon decision learning

0 minutes: Children arrive in class and with no further introduction; start work together.

15 minutes: Stop children and ask a group to say what they have done. Children can then carry on or can change activity.

30 minutes: Decide whether to stop again as a whole class for a mini-plenary, or to talk with individuals or groups about their current and next activities.

1 hour: Start thinking about who will contribute to the plenary; ask target children to prepare.

1 hour 15 minutes: Tell children that they have five minutes to finish what they are doing, or get it ready to leave for a while.

1 hour 20 minutes: Stop the class.

Organise your plenary session around a whole-class dialogue in which you:

- summarise work done, using children's ideas, misconceptions, questions and examples;
- invite children's contributions and presentations;
- reflect on and evaluate curriculum learning;
- reflect on supportive uses of speaking and listening;
- discuss positive and problematic aspects of collaboration for learning;
- ask for questions or suggestions for further work.

1 hour 40 minutes: Ask all children to tidy up, stressing that this is part of their work and learning. Work in progress should be kept for another session. Once tidy, ask groups to complete their planning sheets to say what they have done, and suggest what they want to carry on with or do next.

2 hours: Session ends.

More ideas for successful decision learning

- Before you start, tell children what is going to happen and why. Ask for questions. Talk through feelings – or problems – they expect to experience; help them to realise that they have choices to make when they are annoyed, exasperated or irritated by someone else. Ask for suggestions.
- Emphasise the idea that stopping others' learning will not be tolerated.

- Careful choice of group members can help avoid some friction. Let children have some choice in this – but not complete choice. These are working groups, not friendship groups. Ask every child to give you a slip of paper with two names of good work partners. Keeping these confidential, decide on groups in which each child has chosen at least one workmate.
- Expect children to work in groups to start with. As the time goes on, grouping may change as children 'finish' or choose to join a different activity.
- Establish a class atmosphere of collaboration rather than competition to help children to feel that they are succeeding in their learning because of others, not despite others.
- Make explicit the problems you have of organisation, with 30 children and few adults. Ask them to consider the advantages they gain from education. Help them to realise that they are being offered opportunity, not made to do things. Point out that you recognise the difficulties of, for example, lack of space, lack of resources, having to stay in the same room, so many people, and so on. Find out what they think may hamper learning.
- Remind children that their families want them to do well, and expect them to gain from their time in school; that one of their responsibilities within their family is to do their best in class.
- Discuss behaviour and ask children to decide what problems arise when too many people are not working as expected.
- Organise interesting activities and resources. This is not to say that children should seek and be given constant and novel entertainment. It can ultimately be more satisfying to do one thing well than dip into lots of things. This has to be learned.
- Provide a break table with sand timers – no books or paper or anything; the only 'entertainment' on offer should be the chance to chat with others and have a drink of water. Three or four minutes break can be a good choice for children in intense learning situations.
- Have a physical space for reading, planning, drawing, evaluating. For some children, provide a choice between two activities only; or ask the child to act as observer of others, looking for positive behaviour or skilful work to report in the plenary. Make sure that there is chance to talk and think; this may mean some off-task talk for brief stretches of time, but should never mean that behaviour is inappropriate.

The role of the teacher, Teaching Assistant and child

Once children are engaged with their activity, you can teach individuals and groups what they need to know or understand. Take time to circulate, talk, listen, organise things children need, and intervene with information, suggestions and ideas. Learning happens through children using you, the TA and each other as their best resources; you benefit by gaining opportunities to engage with children's thinking. Find out what they know and want to know. Don't consider yourself a 'facilitator' – your role is much more subtle and powerful – that of teacher, in fact! Help create sensible choices for children, and pre-empt disengagement by keeping an eye on how groups are working and what they have achieved. Ensure all children feel included. As usual, timing is really important but should not be a pressure for the children. They will need to be aware of stopping times a little before they happen. Establish timings in advance and keep an eye on the clock as you go on. While the children work, you can take note of good ideas, discussions, creativity and learning. Suggest ways that children can bring these to the plenary, so that all can see their value and purpose.

Your TA can support your teaching, talking with children about their work, spending time with individuals requiring support, providing input where resources are complex, and helping to settle those who are finding things difficult.

The importance of taking responsibility for learning should be made entirely explicit to children. They should understand how to support others in their group and in the class. They should know that they need to tackle activities wholeheartedly and with concentration, thinking of questions and trying to answer them. In particular, they should be prepared to offer relevant ideas and information. Some children need to be prepared to contribute to the closing plenary session.

Organising a whole day of decision learning (3 hours + 2 hours)

Previous week: Plan and collect resources; discuss ground rules for collaborative work; introduce the topic. Children can research specific aspects of the topic and bring in ideas, questions and resources.

Previous day – ½ hour: Discuss ground rules with reasons; remind about expectations for learning and behaviour. Ask for any thoughts on this. Demonstrate and highlight possible activities. Establish groups; ask children to talk with their group to plan which activity to do first and why. You may want to specify which activities *must* be done some time during the day, and which are optional. If children have had experience of making decisions about learning, they may be ready to settle to activities for an appropriate amount of time without you having to specify a 15 minute minimum; but this may still be necessary for some children.

Morning session

You may need to begin with, or incorporate somewhere, your usual register routine.

0 minutes: Children arrive in class and with no further introduction start work together.

15 minutes: Stop children and ask a group to say what they have done. Children can then carry on or can change activity.

30 minutes: Decide whether to stop again as a whole class for a mini-plenary, or to talk with groups about their current and next activities.

1 hour: Ask target children to prepare contributions for the plenary.

1 hour 15 minutes: Tell children that they have five minutes to finish what they are doing, or get it ready to leave for a while.

1 hour 20 minutes: Stop the class and organise a whole-class discussion:

- a summary of work done;
- children's contributions and presentations;

- reflection and evaluation of curriculum learning;
- reflection on uses of speaking and listening and collaboration;
- questions or suggestions for further work.

Before break time

Provide five minutes reflection time during which children think about what they have done, think about how they have helped others, and how others have helped them. Decide how to overcome problems with work or with social interactions. Make sure that they have a plan in place for after break – the plan can be oral, a picture or written; encourage each child to share with others what they plan to do and why. Re-start those who have lost motivation or have come to the end of a project.

After break

Continue, making sure that some further activities are available.

Plenary: 20 minutes before lunch, stop everyone. Ask children to discuss and show what they have achieved and then nominate others who have found out or made something interesting; who have been collaborative, thoughtful, a good listener – whatever social and educational skills that your class is working on. Decide whether activities will carry on during the afternoon, and if so what extra resources and input will be required. Do the class need a re-start, extra information, access to other ICT, PE session, a trip to the library, a run in the playground?

If decision learning is to continue after the lunch break, ensure that everyone has a plan in place. If there are particular things that children have not done, check that the child plans to tackle them. Again provide one or two new activities or resources for those who thrive on novelty. For those who need more structure, provide specific activities and a helping hand in the shape of yourself, the TA or another child.

After lunch

Children come in and continue working. This session should be kept fairly brief, so that children do not lose momentum and motivation.

Plenary: After about 45 minutes, organise a plenary:

- ask children to set out the day's work at their places; ask everyone to look around the room and evaluate what everyone has actually made, written or produced;
- ask for feedback – positive comment and suggestions;
- ask for children's ideas about their achievement during the day;
- decide what could be done on a further decision learning day;
- think about what the children will do when they arrive in class the following morning; can they come in and get on with something?

Ending the session

Ask children to tidy up and sit down; talk to them about all the good things that have happened in terms of curriculum learning, thinking, collaboration, behaviour. Ask for suggestions for the next session. Finish on a positive note.

Behaviour for learning: and a classroom crime

One barrier to decision learning is the very real worry that children will misbehave, waste time, become over-excited or just hang around claiming to be bored; this is how some children go on, when given some sorts of freedom. However, decision learning is focused on just that – learning – with high expectations for engagement and therefore for responsible and positive behaviour. It is not too difficult for most children to learn this, if they don't know it already. They are quite aware of their own powers, capacity and inclinations; they know what sort of behaviour tends to stop others learning. Shared ground rules can help to ensure that 'freedom to choose' does not become 'freedom to choose to stop others learning'; this is a real classroom crime and can be flagged up as such.

Learning falls away when children behave in unsocial ways. This is especially so when children work with partners or in groups, when they have to wait to use things, when they have to share or organise or create things together – and when they have the chance to make decisions. Difficult behaviour hampers learning. But learning how to get along with others in a purposeful working context is fundamentally important.

We can avoid the problem of trying to teach children how to work with others, by insisting on silence. It's not a bad thing. A quiet classroom, with seated children looking down at their work, is very appealing. It is a special environment in which many children flourish. The classroom will be judged as 'hard-working' by others. You will have control over what is done, said and heard, and it is important that you do. It is a sensible way to go on for some sorts of activities. Peace and quiet enable diligent attention to the task in hand, and it is the teacher's job to create this environment when needed. It can help everyone to feel an unusual sense of calm and orderliness. The hyperlinked out-of-school environment in which children exist offers enough whizziness, distraction, sound and fury; in school we can provide a creative contrast. I am sure that quiet classrooms benefit children. You may have sensed that there is a '. . . but . . .' implicit in this –

A sustainable way to learn

– but if (for now) we take curriculum learning as given, what *other* things do we need children to learn? What is our aim in educating them? I believe that we teach our children in order to help them become independent, resourceful and collaborative people. The capacities to be independent and to collaborate seem to be opposites, but are actually essentially linked. Education should bring out the best in children. It should leave them feeling that they can go out into the world to find out what they want to know, and do what they want to do. Simultaneously it should help them to see that they are highly dependent on other people; and that this dependence carries with it a responsibility for others. As for resourcefulness, children should begin to see that they can learn by following their own aptitudes and interests.

Problems with behaviour

In school, we need children to learn how to settle down to a task, becoming intelligently involved with things and persevering even when things seem to go wrong. They need chances to take responsibility for their own learning and that of others and to collaborate with others, making sensible decisions about what to do and say. We want children to remain curious, channelling their energy into learning. Learning these things in class helps young people to take their place in the world. As attractive as quiet classrooms are, they offer the child few chances for such development. Many children will gain this sort of social learning outside school. Many others will not. Funnily enough, school is the ideal place to learn how to learn when you are not at school. We just need to organise it that way.

Decision learning both depends on and helps to establish co-operation. Talk is the medium through which behaviour is negotiated. What problems might arise? You will not need me to tell you that it is unrealistic to expect complete harmony amongst a group of 30 or so children for a whole afternoon, never mind a whole day. During decision learning children will find one another's actions demanding, difficult, exasperating and selfish. They may act in these ways themselves. How they deal with others – or their perceptions of others – will profoundly influence their chance to learn. A secure and courteous classroom environment can help children to move away from the most destructive aspects of their behaviour, and join those who are not constantly at odds with the world and one another. Children need to discover that they cannot really change the behaviour of others, but they certainly can, and sometimes should, change their own.

Strategies for reflecting on behaviour

- Ask the child to recall and explain reasons for the agreed ground rules.
- Ensure that there is at least one alternative and interesting activity; move the child on to this, with a new partner, TA or alone.
- Provide the child with a clipboard and observation sheet. Ask them to spend two minutes watching each group at work, making a note of particularly interesting talk, collaboration or supportive work. Stop the class for a few moments and ask the child to provide this positive feedback.
- Ask the child to sit at a good vantage point and carefully observe the class for two minutes, then nominate a classmate who deserves 'points'/golden time, etc.
- Spend time talking with the child to devise a new plan.
- Ask the child to account for their behaviour and to make a different choice.
- Ask the child to read quietly, to find or make a page/item/slide which will be useful for the class in the plenary.
- Ask a group to 'invite' the child to work with them for five minutes. Encourage the child by talking about their strengths.

Conclusions

For children, the chance to choose what they will do, coupled with an orderly structure which allows them to share problems with others is an invaluable experience. It is not possible to work this way all the time . . . it is of course possible to work in the usual teacher-directed way all the time – but should it be the only way? Asked why they want to teach, most teachers I have met say it's because they like working with and talking to children. There is no reason why we teachers shouldn't do that, despite the imposition of a crowded curriculum, a punitive external testing regime, and inspections which make judgements based on only what is measurable. We teachers love seeing children learning, developing and thinking, and we need to talk to them. Encouraging children to choose what they want to do helps them to accept responsibility for their own learning experiences, and provides opportunities for some special, individual teaching.

Chapter 8

CREATING A SPEAKING AND LISTENING CLASSROOM

Children need to know how to talk to you and one another, and why this matters for their own learning and that of their classmates. Here is a summary of the conditions that you can create to help children discuss things effectively.

Summary: creating a speaking and listening classroom

Talk about talk for learning with the children.
Teach them what exploratory talk is.
Use exploratory talk yourself when talking with the class.
Use words such as *think, discuss, elaborate, perhaps, why, if –*.
Include time for talk in planning and make sure talk happens.
Always have a speaking and listening Learning Intention.
Help them to agree on, and use, a class set of *ground rules for exploratory talk*.
Listen to children's talk about their ideas, experiences and feelings.
Make sure group work activities offer the right level of challenge.
Ensure that there is always plenty to talk about.
Sometimes organise decision learning in which children choose what to do.
Discuss the impact of talk in closing plenary sessions.
Ask the class to evaluate their group work as well as talking about the topic.
Include talk vocabulary in displays and presentations of work.
Ask children to evaluate their experience of talk in class.

Talking with children for teaching and learning

I would like to finish my book with two contrasting examples of classroom talk. In both, the teacher (who I will call Olivia) was beginning a lesson. She had asked me to help her to think about her talk with the children. She wanted to create a speaking and listening classroom in which she discussed things with the children, and she couldn't quite put her finger on why this didn't seem to be happening. She was not convinced that the children were gaining much from her lesson introductions.

In the first lesson, from which **Transcript 9: The baby clinic** is an extract, children were going to help set up and use a new role play area. After this lesson Olivia and I talked about what she wanted to do to alter the way she and the children discussed things. Three weeks later I visited the classroom again. The children were learning about eggs. **Transcript 10: What can you tell us?** is an extract from the lesson introduction.

In both transcripts, we can use the analysis suggested in Chapter 2:

How many 'teacher's questions' are there?
How much of the teacher's talk is to do with relationships or behaviour?
Does the teacher explain anything?
Does she discuss things with them; is she listening to the children; does she find out what they already know or think?

And importantly, we can think about this:

What did the children learn?

Transcript 9: The baby clinic

T:	OK. We are going to make the role play area into a baby clinic. Baby clinic. Bottoms, legs crossed. What is a baby clinic? Bobby?
Bobby:	A clicky thing.
T:	Not quite. Jamie?
Jamie:	A baby nursery.
T:	Not quite. One more guess then I'll tell you. Jesse –
Jesse:	Where you have a picnic.
Matt:	I know, it's where –
T:	Matt, don't call out and you're not on your bottom that's why I haven't chosen you. OK – Matt?
Matt:	It's preschool.
T:	No. Kevin. Turn around. Stop the shoe noise and face this way. It's a baby clinic where babies get weighed and measured. Mums, Dads and carers take babies to the baby clinic. What can we do in the baby clinic? Callum –
Callum:	You can go on the computer.
T:	Right, well, the receptionist might have a computer, and if you are a patient, she will use the computer. Angel. Shoes. Stop. What are patients? Kya?
Kya:	You wait in a line, if you talk too much, you wait . . . so you're a patient.
T:	Ummm . . . good. Now, what is this for? *(holds up toy stethoscope)*
Bobby:	The dentist.
T:	Oooh, hands up. You've got a good answer but you must put your hand up. *(no hands up)*

Transcript 10: What can you tell us?

T:	OK . . . think. What can you tell us about eggs?
Corrie:	They crack a lot.
T:	Yes! They are very fragile. What can you tell us Kyle?

Kyle:	They are for birds.
T:	Yes, birds lay eggs. Charlize?
Charlize:	Tadpoles.
T:	Tadpoles come from eggs. And what do they turn into?
Charlize:	Frogs.
T:	Frogs, well done. Lukas?
Lukas:	There is Easter eggs, eggs, you can eat eggs.
T:	You can. I've got lots of different eggs to show you. Look at this *(ostrich egg)*. With the person next to you, can you think, umm, tell us, um, where this egg came from? What sort of egg you think . . . *(children talk for 1 minute)* Paolo?
Paolo:	Um, from water, a frog.
Bobby:	It can grow into a giant frog.
Jesse:	Once the frog lays the egg it gets bigger and bigger.
T:	Hmm, a BIG frog! . . . Connor?
Corrie:	It's something that came out of the ground.
Matt:	It used to have chocolate round it.
T:	I see! . . . right well, look, this is a hen's egg – this is *bigger* – so, what *bird* might live in it? *(no replies)* Shall I tell you what it is? An ostrich egg. Do you know what an ostrich is? *(children: yes/no)* Well, um, a big bird. Is it bigger than me?
Charlize:	Yes.
Lyra:	An ostrich can be our teacher.
T:	*(amused)* Oh, well, it might be big enough. Now what do you think came out of this? *(hen's egg)*
Freya:	A chick.
T:	– and this one, a little bit bigger?
Freya:	A bigger chick *(children not making the link between egg size and bird size)*
T:	Ah. This is, it is a *duck* egg.
Oli:	It looks like a swan egg . . . 'cos it's white.
Samya:	It looks like a bacon egg –
T:	I've got more *(holds up a very small mottled egg)* is it another bird?
Jamie:	Yes, a little baby bird.
T:	Shall I tell you? It's a quail –
Charlize:	A whale!
T:	*(smiling)* A *quail*, a little bird. Do you know what that is? *(children: no)* Look here at this picture, it shows us, on the packet.
Lyra:	It looks like an owl – it has the same skin as an owl.
Charlize:	It's fat.
Lyra:	You shouldn't say that.
Charlize:	Yes you can say it at school. *(teacher passes eggs round for children to inspect)*
T:	OK. Can you tell me something that is *different* about all the eggs?
Bobby:	One's a little bit big and the other's . . . small. *(T nods)*
Jesse:	*(ostrich egg)* It feels like a bowling egg.
Freya:	It's cold.
Paolo:	It's soft.
Lyra:	I'm going to be a teacher when I grow up.

Comment

Using the analysis from Chapter 2, we can look at the talk tools Olivia uses. The first number below is the score in Transcript 9, the second number Transcript 10.

Teacher's questions:	5, 5
Relating:	4, 0
Explaining:	2, 9
Discussing children's ideas:	0, 14

Reflecting on the first session, Olivia was worried about her relationship with the children. She thought they were inattentive and 'difficult'. She was a very, very good beginning teacher who had copied a flawed model of teaching which just wasn't working. We discussed her ideas and decided that she would try the following strategies:

a) Plan a series of authentic questions – that is, questions to which she did not know the answer – and ask the children to think and talk about them.
b) Build on things the children said and show she was interested in their ideas.
c) Avoid 'hands up' by giving the children time to discuss things and then asking named individuals to share their group's ideas.
d) Explain things when necessary.

As you can see, it isn't the number of 'teacher's questions' that has changed in the second session, but the amount of explanation Olivia is able to offer – this is real teaching. A striking difference is the teacher's chance to really discuss things with the children. She asks what they think and lets them tell her and each other. And there is no talk about sitting beautifully because the children know they are part of the proceedings – they are asked to talk together – and they want to contribute. You can see and hear learning happening.

Olivia and I, and the class, loved the second session. They learned about the eggs, and Olivia found out what they did and didn't understand. It was the sort of talk she wanted to have with the children.

BIBLIOGRAPHY

Chapter 3

Staricoff, M. and Rees, A. (2006) *Start Thinking: Daily starters to inspire thinking in Primary Classroom.* Birmingham: Imaginative Minds.
Excellent thinking skills starters for the beginning of the day, during registration time.

Chapter 4

Whitebread, D. (Ed.) (2000) *The Psychology of Teaching and Learning in the Primary School.* London: Routledge.
With especial reference to Chapter 3: Managing face-to-face communication in the classroom (John Robertson) and Chapter 4: Communicating well with children (Isobel Urquhart).

Chapter 5

Edwards, S. (1999) *Speaking and Listening for All.* London: David Fulton Publishers.

Palmer, S. (2006) *How to Teach Writing Across the Curriculum at Key Stage 2.* London: David Fulton Publishers.

Warren, C. (2004) *Bright Ideas: Speaking and Listening Games.* Leamington Spa: Scholastic.

Chapter 6

Farrow, S. (2006) *The Really Useful Science Book: Framework of Knowledge for Primary Teachers.* London: Routledge.

Gardner, M. (Ed.) (1960) *The Annotated Alice.* Harmondsworth: Penguin.

ADDITIONAL REFERENCES AND FURTHER READING

Barnes, D. (1992) *From Communication to Curriculum.* Portsmouth, NH: Boynton/Cook.

Dawes, L. (2008) *The Essential Speaking and Listening: Talk for Learning at Key Stage 2.* London: Routledge.

Dawes, L. and Sams, C. (2004) *Talk Box: Speaking and Listening Activities for Learning at Key Stage 1.* London: David Fulton Press.

Grugeon, E., Dawes, L., Hubbard, L. and Smith, C. (2005) *Teaching Speaking and Listening in the Primary School* (Revised third edition)*.* London: David Fulton Publishers.

Loxely, P., Dawes, L., Nicholls, L., and Dore, B. (2010) *Teaching Primary Science: Promoting Enjoyment and Developing Understanding.* London: Pearson.

Mercer, N. and Hodgkinson, S. (2008) Exploring Talk in School: Inspired by the Work of Douglas Barnes. London: Sage.

Mercer, N. and Littleton, K. (2007) *Dialogue and the Development of Children's Thinking.* London: Routledge.

Wallace, B. and Bentley, R. (2002) *Teaching Thinking Skills Across the Middle Years*. London: David Fulton Press.

Wegerif, R. and Dawes, L. (2004) *Thinking and Learning with ICT.* London: Routledge.

WEBSITES

There are quick links to all the websites below on the Thinking Together website.

1. Thinking Together: http://thinkingtogether.educ.cam.ac.uk/
    Also on the Thinking Together website you will find: lots of resources for teachers; download-able resources from this book, e.g. Talking Points and story endings for *Jorian* and *Onyx Quest*; Speaking and Listening research information; further useful links and references related to creating a speaking and listening classroom.

2. *Hyena Stomp* by Frank Stella at Tate online: http://www.tate.org.uk/servlet/ViewWork?workid= 13816

3. Dimensions Creative Curriculum: www.dimensionscurriculum.co.uk

4. Education Oasis: http://www.educationoasis.com/
    Resources which support writing activities when used in conjunction with speaking and listening. For example, see the Graphic Organisers section.

5. Dragons in the Sky: http://www.davidjowsey.com/education.htm
    A comprehensive pack of literacy activities based on the story, referenced to QCA assessment frameworks.

6. The Literacy Trust: http://www.literacytrust.org.uk/index.html

7. Concept maps: http://www.azteachscience.co.uk/code/development/concept_mapping2/index. html
    A useful tutorial about concept maps as visual aids for thought and discussion.

8. Cambridge Primary Review: http://www.primaryreview.org.uk/
    http://www.primaryreview.org.uk/Downloads/Curriculum_report/CPR_Curric_rep_Pt2_Future.pdf
    Within this website, please use the search term 'Speaking and Listening' or see pp. 46 and 53.

9. Rose Review of the Primary Curriculum: http://www.dcsf.gov.uk/primarycurriculumreview/ downloads/primary_curriculum_execs_summary.pdf

10. The Communication Trust: http://www.thecommunicationtrust.org.uk/